Linking Children's Learning with Professional Learning

Impact, Evidence and Inclusive Practice

Jeanne K. Keay
Christine M. Lloyd

SENSE PUBLISHERS
ROTTERDAM/BOSTON/TAIPEI

A C.I.P. record for this book is available from the Library of Congress.

ISBN: 978-94-6091-643-4 (paperback)
ISBN: 978-94-6091-644-1 (hardback)
ISBN: 978-94-6091-645-8 (e-book)

Published by: Sense Publishers,
P.O. Box 21858,
3001 AW Rotterdam,
The Netherlands
www.sensepublishers.com

Printed on acid-free paper

TABLE OF CONTENTS

ACKNOWLEDGEMENTS

We would like to acknowledge the valuable part played by all the education professionals who participated in the research projects or contributed to this book in any way.

SECTION 1

THE CONTEXT

CHAPTER 1

RELEVANCE, RATIONALE AND CONTEXT

This chapter identifies the context in which we make our proposals for a process model that supports users to link their pupils'/students' learning with their own professional learning; it identifies the major themes addressed in the book, provides a rationale for the development of the process model and briefly describes the content of the chapters which follow. The rationale for the book and the recent historical, political and economic factors, which impact upon the issues covered by the book are highlighted in order to provide the context. We believe that the major themes addressed, professional development and learning; inclusive approaches to assessing and identifying pupils' learning needs; the impact of professional learning on pupils' learning and the evidence required to assess that impact, are problematic and complex issues which are of considerable importance to a wide range of professionals working in education. This chapter will provide an initial justification for the critical discussion about these issues and will also define the groups to whom we refer throughout i.e. the education professionals, the pupils, the managers and professional development providers. The central focus of the book, the development and explanation of the process model, which we propose as a tool, which can be used to assist education professionals to address these complex issues in daily practice, is also introduced. While we recognise that this model may not address all aspects of professional development, for example career focused development, we believe that it has the potential to provide effective support for the identification of appropriate development which links directly to pupils' learning.

DEFINITIONS

Before presenting and discussing the rationale for the book and the major themes which are addressed within it, it is important to define and justify some of the terms used throughout as our decisions about their use have informed, and to a considerable extent, shaped and impacted upon the discussion and content.

Education professionals While much research and writing in the area of professional development in education is concerned with, and refers to, teachers and their experiences, we have deliberately employed the term education professionals in this book in order to broaden the scope and application of our work. The definition of this group encompasses all those professionals who engage with children and young people and have a role to play in the development of their learning within the wide range of formal education settings from early childhood to further education. The research which underpins and has informed the development of the process model we propose in the book has been carried out with a range of these professionals including; teachers, managers, learning support staff, early learning staff, special needs co-ordinators and human resource managers, working in a wide range of education settings. These include special and mainstream primary and secondary schools, early childhood centres and colleges. We believe that it is important to employ this wider definition of the education workforce when discussing the impact of professional development on pupils' learning because it recognises the complex nature of learning and teaching processes and the range of actors involved in them. It also recognises the increased demands of recent and current education policy for the development of inclusion and more inclusive practice which has not only led to increased pressure for multi professional collaboration, but has also led to considerable expansion and change in the education workforce to include a range of new learning support roles. It should be noted that while much of the literature and the research carried out on the subject of professional development and its impact on learning, refers to teachers, as mentioned above, the findings and conclusions of this work can be seen to be relevant to our wider definition of education professionals and have therefore been used throughout the book to support and underpin the issues raised and discussed.

The pupil/students/children The broader concept of education professionals which has been adopted has led to a similar broadening of the concept of the groups identified as the end users of the professional learning and development discussed in the book, the pupils or students. We have referred to them, for the most part, as pupils and/or students, in order to emphasise that we are concerned with impact on learning within formal education settings, as defined above. However, as for example in Chapter 3, where wider approaches to learning, which also encompass informal settings, are discussed we have also used the more generic term, children.

The leaders and managers Once again, as a result of adopting the notion of education professionals to include a wider range, the notion of leaders and managers used is also broad. The term manager refers, for the most part, to those who line manage the professionals and who therefore have a vitally important role to play in determining and facilitating access to professional development opportunities. They also have a crucial role to play in the development of a supportive learning culture in the institution, the importance of which is discussed in Chapters 2 and 7 and which underpins and supports the model presented in the book. However it is possible, in larger organisations, that line managers may themselves be restricted in their sphere of influence over these choices and opportunities by more senior managers who determine overarching policy for professional development for the institution at a higher level. As, for example, where the institutional development plan and performance outcomes take precedence over the needs and choices of individuals within the organisation, an issue which is discussed in more detail below and taken up further in Chapters 4, 5 and 9.

The providers Changes to the funding of professional development for education in England in recent years have had a major influence on the provision available and on the providers. Much of the funding available to enable access to professional development opportunities now goes directly to schools and institutions which are responsible for determining and addressing the needs of their staff. As mentioned above these may, of course, be interpreted as the needs of the institution in relation to the institution's development plan rather than the individual development needs of staff, or indeed the learning needs of the pupils/students. Other funding is tied to the implementation of national government initiatives with centrally provided courses and resource materials. This policy has resulted in a situation for many education professionals where they are "... increasingly directed towards fairly instrumental, information-led training, such as briefings on examination syllabi. This training in turn feeds into a school development plan, which is informed by Government objectives and priorities. The training is in effect depersonalised" (Leaton Gray, 2005, p.27).

The funding to provide professional development is allocated for the most part through free market bidding and tendering processes designed to encourage open competition. Traditional providers such as Higher Education Institutions (HEIs) and Local Authorities (LAs), which in the past were funded to provide the majority of professional development, now bid alongside a wide range of others including for example, private education consultancies, which may be companies or individuals; large businesses and institutions from the private sector; and voluntary organisations and government funded bodies from outside education. This has inevitably led to a very diverse range of providers and provision, the impact of which is discussed in much more detail in Chapters 6 and 10. It has also led HEIs and LAs to modify and adapt their provision and has had considerable impact on the way in which professional development is provided and also, inevitably, on the choices available to education professionals. The term providers, as it is used throughout the book, refers to the whole range of agencies and individuals referred to above and the impact they have on provision available and its quality are addressed further in Chapters 6 and 10.

Having clarified and defined who is included when we refer to education professionals, pupils, managers and providers is also important to understand how their work has been affected by external and political contexts when considering their effectiveness and the impact they, and their professional learning and development, have on their pupils' learning. This examination also provides the rationale for the development of the model proposed by this book.

RELEVANCE, RATIONALE AND CONTEXT

Recent and current education policy in England, and indeed in many countries throughout the world, recognises and places high importance on access for all staff to high quality professional development....."A successful 21st century schools system depends on a highly skilled and motivated workforce that consistently performs to the highest standards and engages in effective PD *(professional development)* that secures the skills required to meet known and emerging challenges." (Training and Development Agency (TDA), 2009, p.8). What is perhaps more complex, and certainly creates considerable pressure for education professionals, is the demand, also enshrined in policy, that they should be able to demonstrate evidence of the impact of their professional development on the learning of their pupils. The issue of impact of professional development on practice is not just an issue in England and has also been recognised as problematic internationally in a number of reports, which refer to the difficulties encountered by managers and education professionals (Ingvarson et al., 2005; Timperley et al., 2007: Bubb et al., 2008; Pedder et al., 2008; Darling-Hammond et al., 2009).

A number of questions arise for education professionals as a result of this policy such as

– How do I determine what sort of professional development I need in order to impact on the learning of pupils?
– How can I identify evidence of impact on pupils' learning as a result of my professional development?
– What counts as impact?
– What counts as evidence?
– How will the impact be measured?
– What are the implications for me and for the pupils of these measurements and assessments?
– How can I access high quality professional development, which addresses these concerns?

These questions in turn raise important issues, of course, for the provision and providers of professional development and also for managers, who play an important role in determining access to professional development opportunities for their employees.

Timperley et al., (2007), in a large scale synthesis of 97 international studies concerned with professional development and learning, identify a number of conditions and principles that should be met in relation professional learning and its impact on pupils'/students' learning outcomes. In summary these are:

– The content of the professional learning is challenging and involves new theoretical understanding and implications for practice but also challenges prevailing discourses and is informed by, relevant to and consistent with policy trends and research.
– The professional learning environment provides extended opportunities to integrate new learning through a range and variety of practice oriented activities. Collaboration with colleagues and providers are used to negotiate meaning and relevance to practice.
– There is a supportive professional learning context which provides time, support from external agencies where necessary, opportunities to engage in a variety and range of learning activities, engagement together with a supportive community of practice which supports new ideas and developments and challenges the status quo.

– There is a supportive practice context in which the organisation of the institution is such that professional learning is supported by management and seen as an important factor in pupils'/students' learning and the collective aim is development and improvement.

They also identify that for professional development and learning to genuinely impact on the learning of pupils/students education professionals must be motivated to engage in new learning. "Some of the most powerful outcomes arose when teachers accepted that their practice was not optimising students' learning opportunities." (p.xvi). This synthesis provides a clear message that while, in the studies investigated, a strong link was found between professional learning and that of pupils/students; "Little is known about how teachers interpret available understandings and utilise the particular skills offered during professional learning opportunities, or the consequent impact of these on teaching practice and student outcomes. What is known is that the relationship is far from simple." (op.cit. p. xxiii)

The aim of this book is to investigate and discuss these issues and in particular to seek to illuminate and provide better understanding about the complex relationship between pupils'/students' learning and professional learning in order to improve the learning experiences of both groups and to make them more effective. The book proposes a practical approach, in the form of a process model, which can be used by professionals as part of their daily practice to enable them to focus on key factors in the relationship, starting with the learning, needs and intended outcomes of the pupils/students. Professional learning needs are identified in relation to the needs of the pupils/students and identification of evidence of impact, what form it should take and how it will be collected, is an integral part of the learning needs identification processes. A supportive, enabling learning culture and learning environment in the institution in which the learning takes place are key factors for this model to be used effectively. The model begins with the identification of the learning needs of the pupils/students and of the sorts of evidence required to demonstrate that these learning needs have been addressed. The next stage is the identification of the professional development needs of the teacher seeking to meet these learning needs and to produce the evidence that this has been achieved. This in turn leads to the design of appropriate professional development which addresses the intended impact on both participants and pupils/students and the production of appropriate evidence of that impact. This process model is intended as a tool to assist and support education professionals as they struggle to find answers to the questions raised above and to understand the complex relationship between their own professional learning and that of their pupils/students, but it is also intended as a tool which can be used to challenge, change and develop practice in the area.

The process model has itself evolved through an organic process of developing ideas throughout a number of research projects in this and associated areas of education, over a period of several years, (see Appendix for an overview of our research). Its development has also been further informed by more recent enquiry, reported in Chapters 8 and 9 and 10, carried out with a range of participants working in different education contexts, in England, the Netherlands and Australia, to test and evaluate its usefulness in practice. The research which has influenced the development of the model and which underpins and informs the discussion throughout the book is practice oriented and is informed by grounded theory, critical realist, critically pragmatic approaches which aim to challenge, critically reflect upon and evaluate not only practices in education but also the policies, theories and values which inform them, with a view to developing and improving them. The interactive dissemination of the findings and outcomes of our research through this book and the model it proposes is, we believe, an essential and integral condition of engaging with the research approaches referred to above, because they are approaches which aim, not only to research and enquire into what is currently going on in practice, but also to challenge, to change and to transform practice. The impetus to design the model came, in particular, from the results of research carried out with providers to identify and use a set of indicators of high quality to evaluate professional development provision in the area of Physical Education (PE) and sport, which was commissioned by the Professional Development Board for Physical Education in the UK (PDB-PE), (Keay & Lloyd, 2008a), and is discussed in greater detail in Chapters 6 and 10. During this research it became apparent that providers and indeed participants of the professional development, were in real doubt and expressed considerable concern about, how to measure impact, what constitutes evidence of impact and especially how to demonstrate impact on pupils/students. The development of the model began in response to these concerns but was also informed by practice and research over a number of years in the areas of inclusive education and the development of inclusive practice; professional learning and development; and critically reflective approaches to learning and teaching. These areas, together with the issues of impact and evidence are therefore themes which run throughout the book, and inform, the chapters which follow.

MAJOR THEMES

Inclusive Practice

The central theme of the book is, as the title suggests, learning. The approach to learning which it promotes is determined and underpinned by a commitment to inclusive education and practice, which recognises learner diversity and aims to enable every child/pupil/student, whatever her or his ability, to strive towards reaching her or his full potential. Learning is seen as an interactive dynamic process between pupils/students and the whole range education professionals who support, enable and intervene in that process. This holistic and inclusive approach to learning is concerned with, and relies upon, the identification and negotiation, together with the learner, of learning needs, which are then used to determine achievable, progressive, developmental learning goals. Sensitive and flexible approaches to assessing success and achievement are employed, which lay emphasis on what the learner *can do* rather than what she or he *cannot do* and which encompass a wide and holistic range of learning outcomes. Intended learning outcomes, in addition to goals are, however, understood and agreed by all those engaged in the learning process so that learners are not only motivated but are also challenged by their learning. This approach also places emphasis on providing useful, high quality, informative feedback, not just about whether, but also about how, the identified learning goals have been achieved, which is then used to inform and negotiate the identification of further learning needs, goals and outcomes. Accountability is incorporated into the approach and impact and evidence of impact are seen as essential to the provision of this feedback. To be effective and successful it is essential that all those engaged in the learning process regard themselves as learners and that education professionals seek to identify their own learning needs, goals and outcomes in relation to those of their pupils/students. The approach is discussed in far greater detail in Chapters 2, 3 and 7 and indeed throughout the book and underpins and informs the discussion about professional development and its relationship with, and impact on, pupils'/students' learning. The process model, which is proposed in the book, is informed by and depends upon this inclusive developmental approach to learning but is also designed as a tool, which can assist with and support the development of inclusive practice.

Professional Development

Professional development should be intensive, ongoing and connected to practice (Darling-Hammond et al., 2009), however it is sometimes disconnected from practice or previous learning (Armour, 2010) or genuine need. It is seen by many as merely 'going on a course' and a means to providing quick fix solutions to professional development needs. Managers sometimes perceive it as a one size fits all event, which is used to deal with particular developments and initiatives (Keay, 2006). While professional development is often seen in this way by education professionals, they also claim that they do not value this approach (Pedder, 2007) and that they place most value on an approach which involves "experimenting with classroom practices, working collaboratively, adapting approaches in the light of pupil/peer feedback and self evaluation" (Pedder et al., 2007, p.13). Attempts to define what is meant by terms such as professional development and professional learning are further complicated by the acknowledgment that professional learning and development can take place in a wide range of contexts and that it is necessary to understand the individuals and the social systems in which they operate in order to understand the process of professional learning (Borko, 2004). The definition which informs and underpins the model proposed by this book, which is discussed in much more detail in Chapters 2, 4 and 6, is any activity that consciously aims to improve practice and is a reflective process, embedded in practice. While the definition of what constitutes professional development and learning is a major theme, which runs throughout and informs the discussion, professionals' commitment to understand the importance of, and engage with, professional learning is also crucial. Day and Qing Gu (2010) suggest that teacher commitment is one of the most critical factors in the progress and achievement of students. In their research they found that good teachers also have an enduring belief that they can make a difference to the learning lives and achievements of their students, if teachers are committed to making a difference they must also be committed to their own learning. It is therefore clear that teacher professional development, and indeed the professional development of the whole education workforce, is an important element in ensuring pupil learning.

Reflective Practice and Enquiry

In their synthesis, Timperley et al., (2007) identify the importance of an approach to professional learning which is underpinned by the motivation to change practice, where the professionals view themselves as change agents who adopt an enquiry approach to professional learning.

> "The teacher learning needs inquiry begins by focusing on existing teaching-learning links and the outcomes for students. Having established these it asks teachers to understand what they need to learn and do to promote their students' learning. An essential element of this enquiry is that teachers see themselves as agents of change for their students' and their own learning." (p. xliv).

This enquiry approach to professional learning, which places central importance on the interactive nature of the learning relationship between professionals and pupils/students is key to addressing the questions raised above about impact and evidence. The approach requires that education professionals develop a critically reflective, investigative approach through which they rigorously interrogate and evaluate what they do in practice, the theories and assumptions that underpin that practice and the impact of that practice, with a view to developing, improving, and where necessary, changing it. The value and importance of this approach is summarised in a case study research project, which was implemented to investigate the potential of professional development, underpinned by a model of critically reflective action research and enquiry, to change practice in order to develop more inclusive education (Lloyd 2002).

> The impact identified... by the whole group included changed perspectives about the roles of pupils and teachers in the learning process – the development of self-critical analysis, not just looking critically at the pupils... A more systematic approach to evaluating practice has been developed, as well as a more questioning approach to practice. The importance of stimulating critical discussion with colleagues and a recognition of the value of collaborative reflection, evaluation and sharing experience is identified as a major change, as it putting practice under the scrutiny of others. (p. 125).

Professional development and learning, founded in a critically reflective enquiry approach has long been seen as a powerful and empowering tool for change and development in education (Carr & Kemmis, 1986: Giroux, 1990: Kemmis, 2005). This approach and its significance for education professionals seeking to identify and provide evidence of the impact of their learning on that of their pupils/students is explored throughout the book and has played an important role in the development of the model it proposes.

Impact and Evidence

As mentioned above, increasing importance has been placed in recent years in education in England, and indeed in many other countries (Timperley et al., 2007), on external rather than integral accountability, of the sort described in the earlier section on inclusive learning. The introduction of professional standards, tied to performance management and measured by inspection, has become the chief vehicle for enforcing this model of accountability in England and has led to a strong drive to access professional development which is directly linked to school development plans with the expressed aim of improving the performance of the school. While pupils' learning is clearly a part of this picture, it is often not at the centre of the identification of teachers' professional development needs. Burns (2005), found through education policy analysis that "... references to competencies and school development plans, knowledge and skills, show them to be part of the rhetoric of accountability, a top-down view of how change might be effected..." (p. 354). He explores the tensions created in a system where the individual professional needs of teachers are often subsumed and marginalised in the interests of improving the effectiveness and performance of institutions and the need to provide evidence that this improvement has taken place. These tensions are further compounded by the fact that, as mentioned above, much of the funding for professional development available in England is now school based, tied to the introduction of new government initiatives, is often short term and takes the form of one off days or a short series of training events. Inevitably these pressures give rise to real concern amongst providers of professional development, and education professionals about what counts as impact, how it can be measured and what counts as evidence of impact. Indeed, as mentioned above, in the research which inform this book (Keay & Lloyd, 2008a; Keay & Lloyd, 2008b) the providers and the participants of the provision considered these questions to be paramount amongst their concerns. Pedder (2008) identifies that while there is considerable literature and research focusing on this issue that professional development can improve learning, this is rarely related to pupil achievement and learning. Indeed a review of some recent research about issues relating to impact and evidence of impact (Burchell, Dyson & Rees, 2002; Lyle, 2003; Baumfield & Butterworth, 2005; Burns, 2005; Baumfield, 2006; Ingvarson et al., 2005, Timperley et al., 2007) reveals that while a considerable number of projects have been set up to investigate it, they are, for the most part, concerned with the impact of professional development on teachers, and in some cases other professionals, and their practice and learning and on school improvement and effectiveness rather than on pupils'/students' learning. While there are inevitably changes identified in the learning processes in the classroom as a result of professional development, the issue of measuring the impact of these changes on the pupils'/students' learning is not addressed rigorously by the systematic collection and analysis of data (Timperley et al., 2007) and often relies on making general claims of the causal variety.

Research with professional development providers (Keay & Lloyd, 2008a) revealed that they did not consider children as stakeholders in teachers' professional development and in a national research project investigating teachers being prepared to cascade professional development to colleagues in their local authorities (Keay & Lloyd, 2008b), it became clear that the participants related impact to policy outcomes rather than to children's development. Many professional development providers do not recognise the importance of end-users at all in their provision, it is frequently focused on the needs of participants and the link is not made between the learning of the participants and their pupil/students. In both pieces of research while they acknowledged the importance of recognising the impact of development activities on children, the participants struggled with questions about what counts as evidence of impact and how it might be gathered, issues which are discussed further in Chapter 10.

Burchell, Dyson and Rees, (2002), asking "what constitutes evidence of impact on practice resulting from teachers' engagement in CPD courses?" (p. 219), recognise the importance of producing evidence of the impact on pupils' learning, and make the case for using self reports and reviews by the teacher as important tools for the production of evidence of impact. However, while it is vitally important that education professionals engage in reflective self review on changes to their practice resulting from professional development, since this process can be seen as having an important contribution to make to the process of identifying the impact of professional development on themselves, their institutions and their pupils, this approach often relies on anecdotal evidence and is rarely, if ever, based on a systematic, accurate analysis and assessment of children's and young people's learning needs. Indeed, the Office for Standards in Education (Ofsted) (2006) found that few schools evaluated the impact of professionals' development on teaching and learning effectively and ascribed this to their failure to identify its intended outcomes and to design suitable evaluation methods at the planning stage. It would seem then, that there is a lack of understanding about impact and what counts as evidence of the impact of professional learning on the learning of pupils and students. Questions arise about how pupils' individual and group learning needs are identified, assessed and monitored and whether these processes are adequately embedded in teaching and learning. Issues about the social construction of what we mean by success and achievement and their measurement (Lloyd, 2008) give rise, in turn, to further questions about how changes and developments in learning can be adequately evidenced through improved test results or scores or whether there is a need to look for more qualitative, meaningful data, collected over time, to demonstrate impact. Is impact on learning synonymous with impact on performance or is there a more long term, hidden aspect to impact on learning which may not be overtly demonstrable or easily measured? These issues about impact and evidence are centrally important themes and are dealt with in detail in particular in Chapters 4, 5 and 6 but also throughout the book and have provided the inspiration and the motivation for the development of the process model as a practical tool to support and assist education professionals as they strive to address them.

Having provided an, albeit brief, introduction to the context and the central themes which inform and underpin the book the following provides a brief outline of the content and organisation.

OVERVIEW

The book is divided into three sections:

Section 1   The Context This section provides the rationale for the book and its aims. It highlights the major themes, which run throughout the book and are discussed in the following chapters. (Chapter 1: Relevance, Rationale and Context*)*

Models of professionalism, resulting approaches to, and understandings about, professional development and learning and professional knowledge are discussed and examined critically and readers are challenged to reflect on their own professional learning and its relationship to the learning of pupils/students. (Chapter 2: Professional Development, Professionalism and Professional Knowledge)

Recent and current developments in education policy for inclusion have resulted in increased learner diversity and a range of changed and developing roles for education professionals and have led to increased pressure on learning, teaching and assessment. Issues arising from these increased pressures, and a discussion about inclusive practice in learning, teaching and assessment are discussed. (Chapter 3: Developing Inclusive Approaches to Learning Teaching)

Section 2   Measuring Impact This section addresses what constitutes high quality professional development and how it is impacted upon by the political and economic constraints of policy and the role of impact and evidence in determining quality. It draws on research carried out with providers of professional development and discusses an example of a self-regulated approach to quality assurance in order to challenge readers to consider the role of a professional community of practice in assuring high quality professional development. (Chapter 4: High Quality Professional Development)

A range of research and literature, including our own research, in the area is drawn on to discuss and critically evaluate the impact of professional development and learning. Models of impact driven professional development are discussed and the role of evidence and what counts as evidence in determining impact are critically evaluated. (Chapter 5: Impact of Professional Development)

Impact and evidence are then critically discussed from the perspective of the pupils'/students' learning. Inclusive, process oriented approaches to learning, teaching and assessment, drawing on examples from research, which support and enable the collection of a wide range of qualitative evidence which can be analysed to provide information about impact are explored. (Chapter 6: Learning and Teaching – Gathering Evidence of Impact on Learning)

This section culminates with a description of the development of the process model of impact driven professional development proposed by this book as a tool to support the development of inclusive approaches to identifying professional learning needs in relation to the learning needs of pupils/students and to identifying evidence of impact. The culture and context, which are a pre-requisite for the effective implementation of the model, are also discussed. (Chapter 7: The Model)

Section 3   The Model in Practice This section of the book critically examines how the model can be used most effectively beginning with education professionals. Case studies carried out with a range of professionals in a variety of learning contexts in England, The Netherlands and Australia are used to reflect on the scope and limitations of the model in use. (Chapter 8: Practitioners)

The role of the managers in the implementation of the model and issues impacting on that role are critically examined and the development of a supportive culture and learning environment in which the model can be most effectively used is discussed. Data collected from the case studies mentioned above is again used to provide illustrations and examples of good practice. (Chapter 9: Leaders and Managers).

The wide variety of providers of professional development in education and the opportunities they provide are also considered critically in relation to the model. The need for providers to consider the learning needs of the end users of their provision, the pupils/students, as well as the participants, and to seriously address the issues of impact and evidence through their provision is discussed. The role of the model in supporting these developments is considered. (Chapter 10: Professional Development Providers)

The book concludes with a summary of the main issues presented and a critical analysis of the ideas it promotes and areas that require professional engagement and further research are identified. The challenge is issued to readers to consider and reflect on the use of the process model to assist and support them with the processes of identifying, assessing and providing evidence of the impact of their professional learning on the learning of the pupils/students. (Chapter 11: Conclusion)

CHAPTER 2

PROFESSIONAL DEVELOPMENT, PROFESSIONALISM AND PROFESSIONAL KNOWLEDGE

This chapter examines three related concepts, professional development, professionalism and types of professional knowledge, all of which have an impact on the practice of education professionals in schools and learning centres. These concepts, together with inclusive approaches to learning and teaching, discussed in Chapter 3, underpin the process model we have developed to help education professionals to link their learning with the learning of their pupils/students. It is therefore important to explore each concept and how they interrelate. The first part of the chapter examines professional development, as a concept and as activities in practice, and considers its definition in relation to professional learning. The relationship between two different modes of professionalism and how their characteristics may affect the roles of education professionals and the choices they make about professional development are then explored in part two. In a third part, professional knowledge types and their relationship to professional development is explored. The chapter concludes with a consideration of how the challenges raised through this analysis, which education professionals may encounter in accessing professional development, may be addressed through the adoption of a personalised approach.

WHAT IS PROFESSIONAL DEVELOPMENT?

While the nature and purpose of education professionals' roles is affected by the external political context and associated expectations, their roles are also influenced by the professional development they are offered and the activities they select. There is a general expectation that education professionals will undertake professional development and a cursory review of the expectations of a range of professions supports the view that, in general, professionals are expected to take responsibility to develop in role. For example, the Code of the Nursing and Midwifery Council (2008) in the UK states that members must keep their skills and knowledge up to date; they must have the knowledge and skills for safe and effective practice when working without direct supervision; keep their skills up to date throughout their working lives and take part in appropriate learning and practice activities that maintain and develop competence and performance. These requirements are indicative of general expectations in many occupations that claim professional status. However, while professional development may be a generic expectation of professionals, the detail of how and when it may be undertaken, how it is resourced and what is understood by

15

professional development is not consistent. For education professionals, answers to these questions vary considerably, however, as the discussion below will indicate, there is some consensus about best practice.

Teaching quality has, not surprisingly, been linked to student achievement and Scheerens et al., (2010, p.190) found that research evidence underlined the importance of overall teaching quality as a lever for improving student achievement. The time provided for education professionals to develop has also been linked to the high achievement of pupils and Darling-Hammond et al., (2009) found that:

> A majority of schools in high achieving nations provide time for teachers' professional development by building it into teachers' work day and/or by providing class coverage by other teachers. (p.15)

In some countries, professional development requirements for the teaching workforce are mandatory and there are national statements about how many hours teachers are expected to devote to development. For example, The Netherlands, Singapore and Sweden require at least 100 hours of professional development per year (Darling-Hammond et al., 2009) and in some states in the USA the expectation is tied to job security with a set number of hours required annually if a teacher wishes to continue teaching in a state school. In Luxembourg and Spain, teachers are eligible for a salary bonus if they enrol for a specified amount of professional development (Scheerens et al., 2010). In 2001 in Scotland, the McCrone Agreement set out a contractual statement which required teachers to undertake 35 hours of professional development each year and to keep a log of activities (http://www.gtcs.org.uk/professional-development/cpd.aspx). However this time requirement is not widespread, and in England, for example, while the Professional Standards Framework (TDA, 2007) states that teachers should take responsibility for identifying and meeting their professional needs, the measurement and recording of professional development, while it occurs in some schools, is not a legal requirement. A cross party Select Committee Report on the training of teachers in England (2010) has, however, suggested that a clear expectation is written into teachers' contracts:

> We recommend that a single, overarching 'Chartered Teacher Status' framework, linking professional development, qualifications, pay and the licence to practise, be introduced as a means of structuring teachers' career progression. (p. 6).

While this is a bold move, the report also recognises that issues relating to resources and infrastructure must be addressed to ensure that the requirement can be met.

Implementation of the professional development process model we present in Chapter 7, and on which we have based our recent research, requires a clear understanding and definition of professional development. Terms frequently used by practitioners, policy makers and writers include continuing professional development (CPD), which describes the expectation that learning is a continuous process, and professional learning, which we see as going beyond development to describe what is actually achieved through professional development. However, in discussions with colleagues from outside the United Kingdom (UK), it has become increasingly clear that there is widespread use of the term professional learning in place of professional development. This is particularly so in Australia where the meaning of professional development is linked to a view of learning activities which are enforced and the term professional learning is used to emphasise a different interpretation, where education professionals have professional autonomy over their development. Parr (2010) provides a helpful overview of contrasting understandings of professional development and professional learning in which they are positioned as contrasting discourses. He examines the issue by using the terms managerial understandings of professional development and alternative understandings of professional learning. A summary of the contrasting issues will be used later in the chapter when examining the impact of different professionalisms on professional development. The term we have decided to use is simply professional development and while the term used is not necessarily important, understanding its definition and the practical applications of the definition are, we believe, very important.

Professional development is described, defined, offered, delivered and undertaken in different ways and different labels and categories are used to describe and analyse it; a review of definitions and explanations in literature exemplifies this. For example, Helsby (1999) identifies three categories of development, initial teacher education (ITE), externally provided courses and work-based events, while Eraut (1994) uses the terms continuing professional education (CPE) and CPD to distinguish between external courses and conferences (CPE) and work-based opportunities (CPD). Bolam's (1999) description of CPD as education, training and job embedded support suggests a definition that recognises different elements of professional preparation and development. Darling-Hammond et al., (2009) provide a more qualitative explanation of professional development as intensive, ongoing and connected to practice, while Friedman and Philips (2004) see it as a way of keeping up to date and building a career. An amalgamation of Day's (1999) definition, where professional development is seen as all natural learning experiences and conscious and planned activities, and Billet's (2001) view of it as a process of reflection and action provides a broader view of the nature of the professional learning process. This broad definition stresses the deliberate nature of the learning process and emphasises that 'natural learning' experiences also need to be recognised and understood by participants as part of the process of learning. There are many informal opportunities when learning takes place during the school day, for example, informal discussions with a colleague in the staffroom, or when trying out different teaching approaches and sometimes making mistakes, or a chance observation of good practice by a colleague. This flexible and wide-ranging approach to professional learning was important for us to acknowledge as we developed the process model. Through a process, which requires reflection on the activity, in the activity and requires action as a result of the reflection, those unplanned learning experiences can become part of learning, a process that is addressed in more detail later in this chapter.

While theoretical definitions of professional development are important to acknowledge as we move towards proposing a process model for professional development, it is also important to understand what development activities are taking place in schools and learning centres. Kennedy (2005) provides a useful overview of the key characteristics of different types of professional development and how they may support transmissive and/or transformative learning activities. She includes training, award-bearing, deficit, cascade, standards-based, coaching/ mentoring, community of practice and action research models in her list. However, Doecke, Parr and North (2008) in a national mapping of professional learning in Australia provide a commentary on changes in professional development practice over the last eight years. They found that professional learning is:

– now seen to be a crucial lever for school and system-wide educational reform;
– integral to the professional lives of teachers;
– being shaped by standards-based reforms;
– dynamic, collaborative and generative;
– grounded in local school communities;
– involves an enhanced role for universities;
– involves practitioner enquiry.

While this list was generated in Australia, we believe circumstances elsewhere would not generate a significantly different list (cf. Darling-Hammond et al., 2009; Pedder et al., 2008). Timperley et al., (2007), in their analysis of research in relation to the New Zealand context, found that teachers engaged in a range of activities and the only activity, which was consistent across the research reports was, listening to others with greater expertise. However, this activity was not undertaken in isolation and was supplemented with multiple opportunities to learn through a spectrum of activities. Their overview identifies that there were positive and negative outcomes for each of the activities reported and supports the view that professional development should be accessed through a range of activities, with success dependant on factors other than the activity itself.

Naturally, definitions and preferences alter according to role expectations and the responsibilities and understanding of the person defining the concept. For example, many teachers define professional development as going on a course and Pedder et al., (2008) found in their State of the Nation Project that the professional development teachers take part in most frequently reflects passive forms of learning such as listening to a lecture or presentation. However, as Armour (2010) points out, such experiences are likely to be disconnected from previous learning. Definitions also affect professional development opportunities provided, for example, managers who have themselves to ensure that organisation level targets are met are likely to provide development opportunities which ensure a whole school/centre approach to particular issues through in-service education and training (INSET), a term which is used to describe a type of professional development provided in-house and driven by organisation development targets. School leaders show a clear preference for professional development that focuses on school-based and classroom-based opportunities as they are seen to provide more value for money (Pedder et al., 2008). While many of these types of professional development appear to be focused on pupil learning, in reality they are merely serving organisation performance objectives. One such example is the sort of teacher research, sometimes leading to an academic award, which is often funded and supported by a school/college management team and where the focus may not be chosen by individual teachers or be essential to their professional development but is entirely focused on school targets. The same can be seen when policy makers provide professional development, often for selected individuals whose responsibility is to cascade the information to their colleagues, in order to ensure that a particular approach is followed (e.g. the professional development to support the National Strategies in England). Of course, the commercial providers of professional development also have an influence and we often see them provide isolated development episodes, with no follow up with participants, which provide a good day out for participants and as long as the venue and lunch are adequate, providers receive positive evaluations (Keay & Lloyd, 2009). While it is possible to simply be critical of such opportunities, they do provide the chance for participants to meet other staff interested in similar issues and can provide opportunities for collaboration and the extension of a learning community. There are also commercially provided resource-led professional development opportunities, which can be of benefit if offered as part of an ongoing support package linked to resources (Keay & Spence, 2010). However, research, which examined the effectiveness of two examples of such professional development, also highlighted that these development opportunities need to be contextualised to participants' own organisations and need to include pupils in the learning experience (ibid). The definitions above describe professional development undertaken through specifically designed events, however, there is also a great deal of literature that examines work-based professional development.

Different approaches to work-based learning have been developed and researched by those interested in this form of professional development and the processes of collaboration, mentoring and coaching are particularly popular. In England, this form of learning has been promoted through policy for over a decade as, for example, in the Department for Education and Employment (DfEE) CPD Strategy (2001), which promoted school-based professional development, claiming that many teachers find that the best professional development comes through learning from and with other teachers. Research by Garet and colleagues (2001) supports this view, as they found that traditional (off site) forms of professional development did not provide the same support or opportunity for teachers to integrate their new learning into practice as reform (integrated into practice) activities did. Teachers inevitably meet difficulties in applying new learning back in school when externally provided professional development activities and opportunities are not contextualised to their own work place (Keay & Spence, 2010). There is also a conflict where off-site courses, selected according to individual development needs, may not match school priorities and therefore make integration into practice difficult. However, while it may be tempting to support a view of professional development that appears to marginalise external sources of learning, we must also recognise that school based opportunities may lack the challenge and creativity that engaging in externally provided professional development can bring. Denying access to a range of development opportunities in favour of only school-based professional development will inevitably limit professional development. Indeed, the latest version of the Training and Development Agency's (TDA) views on professional development (*The Strategy for the Development of the Children's Workforce in Schools, 2009–2012*, 2009) recognises the need for a balance between work-based learning and the use of external expertise in planning and providing development opportunities for the children's workforce.

Work-based professional development requires an approach, referred to as reflective practice, and reflection and analysis of practice are seen by many as having a central role in development. Schon's (1987) term, the reflective practitioner, has been used to encourage teachers and indeed all education professionals to be more than technicians and to reflect *in* action and *on* action. However, there have been critiques of this work (Day, 1999; Beckett & Hagar, 2002), which suggest that reflection may not always produce development and maintain that it is possible to be reflective but ineffectual: "so encouraging teachers to be reflective practitioners (whatever that may mean) may be limiting them to the confines of their personal knowledge and to private engagement with it" (Hoyle & John, 1995, p.76). Larrivee (2000) adds the same warnings about teachers' beliefs being self-generating and often unchallenged, however, she suggests that if teachers develop the practice of critical reflection this will help to avoid being trapped in "unexamined judgements, interpretations, assumptions and expectations" (p.293). Day and Qing Gu (2010) suggest that reflectiveness is an essential component in effective teaching, however, we must clearly go beyond mere reflection in order to activate learning and learning from practice undoubtedly requires a more challenging and skilful form of reflection if it is to result in development. Undertaking a process of reflection may be described as *reflecting in action*, that is, during practice; *reflecting on action*, that is, after a teaching activity; and subsequently taking *reflexive action* as a result of reflecting in and on action. We believe that this process is important as it can ensure that the unintended and unplanned professional development that happens in our everyday professional lives becomes a recognised element in the learning process. Reflecting on practice can make unplanned learning a valuable part of a process of professional development. While such learning may have been unintended, it becomes a valued professional development activity because through reflective practice it is recognised as learning. Planning for future professional development can then take account of this learning in the same way as it would with any other development activity.

What then is professional development and what are the activities we are referring to when we talk about development for education professionals? To summarise the points raised above, the model we have developed, researched and present in this book promotes and is underpinned by the view that professional development is a planned process. Two concepts of professional development, evident in literature and raised earlier in this section, focus on externally provided professional development and informal processes of learning. Hodkinson (2009) suggests that they intersect in Schon's (1987) writing on reflective practice and that: "for a significant period both literatures used these ideas to escape technically rational assumptions of planned learning" (ibid, p.159). As highlighted in the previous paragraph, we are emphasising here that all professional development, whatever the mode, should be part of a planned process.

Professional development consists of a range of activities, which may be school based or externally provided, but will be contextually valuable and relevant to the institution, to the education professional and to the pupils' learning in that school/centre. However, it must be recognised that all education professionals do not learn from the same experience and therefore the process of professional development must be personalised. In using this term we do not infer that learning should be an isolated experience but, as examined later in this chapter, it should focus on and build on individual need.

Professionalism and Professional Development

Professionalism can be seen as a framework within which professionals operate and different modes of professionalism, imposed or adopted, can affect how they operate and develop. Therefore, it is important to examine professionalism and its relationship to professional development and how different modes will affect professional development definitions and subsequent actions. Early literature identifies professional development as a trait of professionalism (Hoyle, 1969), while later literature takes the analysis further and suggests that the nature of professional development depends on the form of professionalism adopted (Hargreaves & Goodson, 1996; Sachs, 2001, 2003). The process of professionalisation has further implications for a definition of professional development and this will be considered in an analysis of control, explored in more detail in Chapter 5.

Previous literature has highlighted disagreements on the meanings of the terms in this field, which is full of overlapping distinctions and debates around professionalism, profession, professionalisation and professionality (Gerwirtz et al., (2009). It is not our intention to enter into a discussion about such definitions in this chapter, and we will confine ourselves to discussing two competing definitions of professionalism and how they affect professional development. We do recognise that embedded in these definitions are references to struggles over ownership and knowledge and later in this chapter different types of professional knowledge, are considered.

In a previous exploration of professionalism (Keay & Lloyd, 2009) we developed Sachs' (2003), Kennedy's (2007) and Evetts' (2003) ideas to examine the relationship between professionalism and responses to quality assurance and here we extend this analysis to look at how two different versions of professionalism affect professional development. Each of these writers has identified similar dichotomous versions of professionalism, which have helped us to examine how the characteristics of each version may affect aspects of professional development.

Sachs (2003) presents two versions of professionalism, which she states have emerged in response to particular social, political, economic and cultural conditions and *old* and *new* forms of professionalism are seen to exist in a context of struggle for dominance. New professionalism is called transformative or democratic and characteristics of her old professionalism can clearly be contrasted with the notion of transformative professionalism (Sachs, 2003). At the heart of transformative professionalism is the need for an inward and outward focus, in which professionals understand themselves and the society in which they work. Other characteristics include collaborative and collegial activity, self-regulation and practice, which is enquiry driven and knowledge building. In comparison, characteristics of old professionalism include conservative practices, self interest, external regulation, contexts which are slow to change and adopt reactive responses to challenges. Kennedy (2007) summarises previous work in the field and identifies two contrasting models of professionalism, managerial and democratic. A managerial conception of professionalism values effectiveness, efficiency and compliance with policy. In explaining democratic professionalism, she draws on Sachs' (2001) explanation of 'new' professionalism, valuing an inclusive approach and self-regulation, which contrasts with systems that are externally imposed and she also emphasises the importance of collaborative action in achieving this form of professionalism. Evetts (2009), in shifting the focus from concepts of profession and professionalisation to professionalism, has identified two 'ideal, typical' views of professionalism and uses the terms *organisational* and *occupational* in relation to knowledge-based work. The same issues of control, authority, and accountability are evident in her analysis, however, other issues relating to decision-making and performance review are also included and are pertinent to the focus of this book and the impact of professional development. The following table summarises the work of these writers and relates their views of professionalism to professional development and combines their ideas with our views about forms of professionalism and their effects on professional development.

Table 1. Professionalism and professional development

Managerial Professionalism (old, organisational)	Aspects of professional development	Democratic Professionalism (new, transformative, occupational)
External regulation	Control	Self regulation
Compliance with policy	Authority	In / out focus
Slow to change, reactive, conservative practices	Decision making	Collaborative, collegial, within an ethical code of practice
External assessment	Performance review	Critically reflective practice
Self interest (organisation and individual)	Motivation	Pupil-centred
Efficiency, effectiveness	Focus	Inclusive, enquiry driven, knowledge building

This analysis can be extended by using Parr's (2010) dichotomy of managerial professional development and alternative forms of professional learning to explain how the two different versions of professionalism lead to different approaches to professional development. It is possible to see that, in a culture adopting a managerial approach to professionalism, a reactive approach to professional development is likely to be the outcome. This results in fulfilling official requirements, meeting targets set by managers, being accountable through standards-based assessment and providing evidence of success. Learning is seen to be generic in nature and professional knowledge is provided as a remedy for problems. In contrast, adopting a democratic model of professionalism leads to a much more proactive approach in which professionals set their own standards and targets and automatically collect evidence that they have been met as an essential part of professional practice. Teachers collaborate in their own learning to create a culture of critical enquiry and professional knowledge is contextual and draws on academic and practice-based research and theory to review and critique practice.

An approach to professional development that requires compliance is very different from one that encourages participation and promotes ownership of the process by the participants. This discussion is developed further in Chapter 5, where an examination of control in relation to the impact of professional development is presented. The model we present in this book promotes an approach that reflects democratic professionalism.

Professional Knowledge

Closely linked with the concept of professional development is that of professional knowledge, which is also a trait of professionalism (Danaher, Gale & Erben, 2000). If the purpose of professional development is to maintain and extend teachers' professional knowledge (Day, 1999), it is important to undertake an analysis of how professional knowledge is understood. However, the task is complex, not only because of the contestability of the construct, but also because of the wide variety of theoretical models used to explain and describe it (Hoyle and John, 1995). Despite earlier views (Lortie, 1975; Jackson, 1968) there seems to be no doubt in more recent literature on the topic, that there is a consensus that professional knowledge for teaching exists (Day, 1999; Eraut, 1994; Hoyle & John, 1995).

If professional knowledge is intended to enable education professionals to perform tasks, roles and duties well (Eraut, 1996), it is important to know the nature of the professional knowledge required to meet such expectations. For education professionals, professional knowledge can be viewed in two ways, firstly 'how' the role is undertaken (the pedagogy) and secondly 'what' is being taught (the curriculum). A review of literature provides many different descriptions of professional knowledge and writers use a variety of descriptions to capture their views about how professional knowledge is constructed, who constructs it and for what purpose. Through an analysis of this literature it is possible to identify four types of professional knowledge: *expert, craft, pedagogical* and *political*

(Beck, 2009; Schulman, 1986; Hiebert et al., 2002; Day, 1999; Hegarty, 2000; Tickle, 2000; Eraut, 1994; Hoyle and John, 1995). Particular types of professional knowledge influence and inform professional development choices and the risks associated with engaging in one particular form of professional development and thus possibly limiting the type of professional knowledge gained, which not only affects the individual but will also have an impact on the learning of her/his pupils. A brief overview below highlights the links between the different types of professional knowledge and professional development.

Expert professional knowledge brings with it the notion of learning from an expert and the format of professional development activities is based on this form of knowledge (e.g. courses, books, lectures) and can address both the *how* to teach and *what* to teach questions. However, this form of professional knowledge is limited if it does not provide the opportunity to put new learning into practice.

Craft professional knowledge promotes learning through apprenticeship, within an education context; it is practical knowledge, relevant to the individual and learned in context. However, it brings with it the dangers of merely perpetuating current practice (e.g. learning by doing or by accepting practice based on cultural norms). It should be recognised, as Hufton (2000) suggests, that, "there may also be some tendency to overemphasise the personally unique and tacit, if not ineffable, features of professional knowledge" (p.241). Another aspect of this type of professional knowledge is suggested by Day (1999), who in his division of knowledge links competence with basic achievement. This form of professional development is seen when teachers report learning by accident, learning on the job or learning by doing; they are learning episodes which focus almost entirely on practical development and the practice of skills without reference to *expert* knowledge/theory, generated through research, for example.

Pedagogical professional knowledge could also be termed pedagogical content knowledge (Schulman, 1986). Schulman used the term to link subject knowledge and pedagogical knowledge to emphasise the need for both theoretical and practical knowledge and emphasises the importance of the relationship. This professional knowledge type links expert and craft types and demonstrates that a teacher needs not only externally generated knowledge and experiential knowledge separately, but also needs to amalgamate them. This is process knowledge and is seen to represent knowledge that determines capability, and goes beyond competence (Day, 1999). The relationship between formal, research validated knowledge, constructed by academics and the action-related world of practitioners is central to the definition of professional knowledge (Hoyle and John, 1995). This form of knowledge draws *expert* and *craft* together and teachers may engage in collaborative activity or action research to explore this form of learning.

A fourth type, *political knowledge*, questions the construction of professional knowledge and is important in the current climate where research generated knowledge is challenged and policy determined by governments plays such a large part in the training and development of those working in education. Knowledge that is constructed politically, economically and socially is of a different order from expert, craft and pedagogical knowledge. This fourth type of professional knowledge, generated through policy and validated in inspection reports, provides received wisdom about what is effective practice and therefore professional development becomes focused on this aspect. A recent example of this form of knowledge, in England, is the promotion of phonics as a main approach to teaching reading. Government commissioned summaries of literature and their subsequent use prompts questions about the selectivity of knowledge and use of the findings as is the case in the phonics example cited above. The case for a link between teaching and research in professional development and the call for teaching to be a research-based profession (Cordingley, 1997; Hufton, 2000) has long been made by educationalists, however, a government department making such a call brings a different interpretation to professional knowledge.

Theories drawn from Bernstein's work offer another way to explore the fourth professional knowledge type and Beck's (2009) analysis is also particularly useful. For Bernstein, the core of any pedagogical discourse involves a re-contextualisation of knowledge, that is, knowledge created in specialised fields of knowledge production (Beck, 2009). Bernstein (1996) identifies two re-contextualising fields that help in understanding types of professional knowledge, the official re-contextualising field (ORF) created by the state and its agents and ministries and the pedagogic re-contextualising field (PRF) created by teachers in schools (*craft* knowledge), departments of education in universities, independent research foundations, specialist journals (i.e. *expert* knowledge). If PRF independently influences ORF there is seen to be autonomy in the system, however, if ORF selects the knowledge to match its policy objectives, to use in its re-contextualisation of professional knowledge, it remains ORF and some forms of knowledge are privileged over others. Beck uses this approach to analyse the English standards for teachers (TDA, 2007) and promotes a slightly different view of them from Furlong et al., (2000), in that while he agrees that the standards, are technicist and performative in nature, he suggests that they do require complex expertise and extensive domains of knowledge and understanding. However, the knowledge required is selected and delivered, especially to new recruits to the profession, and he uses the term trainable expertise to suggest that there is a clear element of control over the knowledge they gain. He suggests that this form of professional knowledge does rely on *expert* knowledge but adopts an assumed common sense approach to the content of the standards, selectively borrowing management theories and what he refers to as a 'loose form of behaviourism'. Types of professional development linked to this are usually drawn from the expert model, with preference given to particular elements of knowledge and learning encouraged through Government funded workshops or resources.

The process model presented in this book can be enhanced and underpinned when professionals use the typology presented above to consider the nature of the professional learning experiences they have chosen, or which have been imposed or made available. We have used this typology with education professionals on postgraduate courses and found that the most dominant form of professional development they cite is concerned with *expert* knowledge. In common with research cited earlier some do not see professional development as anything other than courses and others do not count practical modes of learning as valuable professional experiences. They found it useful and enlightening to consider and reflect upon their professional learning in the terms presented in the typology. Theories about what constitutes professional knowledge not only affect views of professional knowledge but also affect how education professionals define their roles and what professional development is subsequently selected. If it is accepted that professional knowledge can be seen as different types: *expert*, *craft*, *pedagogical* and *politically* constructed, these elements can be seen to form the focus for professional development provision and consequently providers should be aware of what forms of professional knowledge their development activities promote. The challenge for those managing or providing professional development opportunities is to ensure that professional knowledge is integrated with participants' unique, personal and contextual worlds.

Personalisation of Professional Development

In the final section of this chapter we bring together the issues raised in relation to forms of professional development, how adopting different forms of professionalism can affect them and how different types of professional development promote different types of professional knowledge. This section begins to draw together the issues raised in this chapter about professional learning, which will also be addressed further when considering pupil learning in Chapter 6, and suggests that in order to meet pupils' learning needs education professionals' learning should be personalised.

Personalised learning has become an important and popular focus in education policy and has been applied particularly to children's learning (e.g. *Every Child Matters*, DfES, 2004; *2020 Vision*, DfES, 2006). It is not only promoted in England but can also be found in much current policy throughout the world (Beach & Dovemark, 2009). It provides a 'powerful policy rhetoric' (Mahony & Hextall, 2009), which aims to persuade parents (and other politicians) that state schools are able meet individual learning needs of all pupils and provide an appropriate and relevant education for every child. This rhetoric can be identified, and is used extensively, in policy to promote and the drive towards inclusion and to underpin the notion of inclusive practice in education, which is discussed further in Chapter 3.

In the quotation below, Pring (2008) summarises the meaning of personalisation in relation to children's learning:

> learning to be connected to what learners already know and experience; learners monitoring their learning and identifying the next steps; shifting the balance from class levels to individual progress; recognising and respecting the learner's voice; providing out of classroom support and advice; involvement of parents; recognition of non-cognitive factors and higher order thinking skills; provision of different pathways and extension of choice; developing greater self awareness (p.679)

His points can also be applied to adult professional learning. If applied to professional development, personalisation suggests a professional learning process which takes account of prior knowledge, involves reflection on practice, is focused on providing for the individual and respects and expects her/his views and is provided within a flexible framework based on individual need and choice. However, this is a very different model of provision from that in place in the majority of schools and education institutions at present and, as discussed in Chapter 6 in relation to children's learning, we should be very clear that our use of the term 'personalised' relates to a process that addresses individual needs, which are themselves focused on improving children's learning. We acknowledge the political issues around the term personalisation (Leadbetter, 2004) and its application in policy as stressed in the discussion in Chapter 6, but what is being proposed here is personalised learning.

While education professionals experience INSET, where the focus is determined by school targets, and take part in government funded development opportunities, in previous work we found that new teachers, professional development providers (Keay, 2009) and more experienced teachers (Keay & Spence, 2010) saw the purpose of professional development very much as an individual issue. The choices they made about professional development engagement were justified purely in relation to individual need, which may be due to their definitions of organisational or institution led learning activities as not necessarily relevant to their personal needs. They may only define the development activities they have selected as professional development. Education professionals do want professional development to be contextualised so that it makes sense to them in their own working context but they also want it to be personalised to their own needs so that they feel they are not wasting their time or conversely not feeling that they do not have the pre-requisite knowledge to be able to participate in a particular learning experience (ibid). This is a huge challenge for all education professionals, professional development providers and school managers when looking at the issue of providing high quality professional development, as discussed further in Chapter 4.

The notion of personalising professional development for education professionals is linked to the need to contextualise professional learning, that is, to situate learning in familiar contexts, exemplifying activity with pupils who will be involved in learning in these contexts. However, personalised learning goes beyond contextualised learning and the implications for implementing personalised professional development are enormous. In a recent research project, participants raised the issue of meeting personal needs, pointing to differentiated approaches to professional development, which acknowledge prior learning and provide a continuum of support (ibid). They were particularly concerned to ensure that professional learning opportunities were offered in different ways and at an appropriate pace in order to enable all participants to benefit from the learning activity. This has implications for the type and format of the professional development and challenges whether it can deliver personalised learning opportunities.

To achieve a model where personalised professional development is an expectation for all education professionals requires a clear understanding of what it entails. For example, is it merely a deficit model through which to ensure a common level of expertise and knowledge? That is, the learning is the same, the professional development activity is the same but it is undertaken at different times, according to perceived need. Is it a model that merely provides a structure and while individuals have choice, it is limited to the outcomes decided by the institution or indeed the government of the day? Underwood and Banyard (2008) writing about personalised learning in schools (for pupils) and reporting on the outcomes of discussions with an expert panel define it as a desirable state, which should be available to all, giving a degree of autonomy and ownership of learning but within a framework from which core learning goals emerge. This description sounds very much like the Professional Standards Framework (TDA, 2007), in place in England, which is used to inform the development needs of teachers and other education professionals and can be seen to be a deficit model. While such a model clearly has the interests of pupil learning at its heart, it does not acknowledge the specific individual needs of teachers in relation to their pupils. Choice of professional development beyond this model relies on a culture that encourages reflection and dialogue where an institutional professional development framework is in place to support need and identification of need.

A range of similar terms, such as individualised learning, person-centred learning or self regulated learning have been used to describe learning which focuses on individual need and in common with the term personalised learning suggest a process in which the individual has some control. However, this may not always be the case, as education professionals may not have the power to exert influence over the focus or type of their own development activity. Hartley (2009), discussing the idea of voice in relation to children's learning, suggests that personalised learning provides the opportunity for individuals to have a voice in deciding their own learning. If taken in relation to education professionals, this suggestion assumes that each individual has the skills and knowledge to identify professional need and is operating in a professionally reflective way, which may not, in fact, be the case.

If professional development is to be personalised change is necessary, not only in the way most education professionals view development but also in the way providers of learning opportunities develop their provision. They will need to know and take account of individual needs and the one size fits all type of event will require critical revision. Personalised professional development must inevitably take into account professionals' needs in relation to the needs of the children with whom they work, so pupil learning must be clearly linked to any provision. Personalised professional learning requires a different support structure within a culture that acknowledges and addresses individual need as well as institutional need.

CHAPTER SUMMARY

This chapter has examined professional development and two competing frameworks of professionalism within which education professionals work and learn and analysed the nature of professional knowledge and its impact on professional development.

To summarise, professional development can be seen as a range of activities, which are planned, relevant, contextualised, personalised and influenced by the form of professionalism adopted or imposed. The professional knowledge gained is determined by, and determines, the activity and the operational framework.

> A different approach to enhancing teacher learning is required, one that maximises learning potential within the practice of teaching by improving opportunities to learn, incentives to learn and support for learning. (Hodkinson, 2009, p. 164)

The relationships between the learning of education professionals and children's learning is at the heart of the model presented in this book. Professional learning must be embedded in practice and that means learning that has an impact on pupils' learning and the identification of its impact and production of evidence must be part of the process. Chapters 3, 4, 5 and 6, engage with the difficulties in measuring the impact of different modes of professional development on children's learning.

DEVELOPING INCLUSIVE APPROACHES
TO LEARNING AND TEACHING

This chapter addresses a major development in education policy in recent years which has far reaching implications for the daily practice of the whole range of education professionals and for their professional development needs and choices. The drive towards inclusion and the development of inclusive practice have, in recent years, become major imperatives for education policy not just in England, but throughout the world (Pijl, Meijer & Hegarty,1997; Dyson, 1999; Barton & Armstrong, 2008; Armstrong, Armstrong & Spandagou, 2010). This development has been inspired and driven by the United Nations in a number of declarations promoting education for all and the rights of people with disabilities (1990, 1993, 2000, 2006) and in particular by the 1994 Salamanca Statement and Framework for Action on Special Needs Education (UNESCO). These powerful driving forces have impacted considerably as stimulants for educational change and development throughout the world and have led to inclusion and the development of inclusive practice becoming an increasingly important policy agenda and a major challenge for education professionals in practice. In England, and in many other countries throughout the world, these developments have also impacted considerably upon the organisation and provision of education and created major ramifications for the practice and professional development of the whole range of education professionals. It also places emphasis on education professionals' capacity to effectively identify and address pupils' learning needs. The chapter concludes by highlighting four crucial areas, discussed throughout this book, which must be addressed in order to support education professionals to deal with these changes and developments in education policy and practice; Initial Teacher Education (ITE) and professional development; critically reflective practice; practice oriented research and collaboration.

INCLUSION

Inclusion, framed initially in much early policy such as the Warnock Report (DES 1978) and the 1981 Education Act as integration, can certainly be identified as a major priority in education policy over the past twenty or thirty years in England. Within this policy there has been a clear attempt to move away from the traditional medical, deficit models of SEN with provision in segregated schools and classes, where the aim of education was remediation or 'treatment', towards what can be seen as a contextual or social model (Oliver 1992; Barton 1995; Dyson, 1999; Lloyd, 2000), which recognises the potential of the learning context, and indeed of society, to exacerbate or even create special educational needs (SEN). This demands a different approach to the identification and assessment of children's learning needs and to the educational provision made to address those needs which has led, in practice, to a gradual, but extremely slow, move away from the idea that the child is him/herself deficit in some way or requires some sort of quasi medical diagnosis, to an approach which recognises the need to provide extra support for, and to differentiate, learning and the learning context, in order for the child to be educated alongside his/her peers. This in turn puts pressure on education professionals in terms of their ability to identify, assess, address, monitor and evaluate children's learning needs and requires that they are equipped with a range of flexible learning and teaching strategies. The discussion in Chapter 2 about approaches to professional learning and professionalism can be seen, then, to have major implications for the type of professional development required to support the implementation of such major education reform.

The policy for inclusion and the development of inclusive practice has also been accompanied by a growing recognition that in order for children identified with SEN to have an equal educational opportunity they should be receiving their education in the mainstream of education provision and this is reflected clearly in policies, in England, such as the Green Paper, *Excellence for All children; Meeting Special Education Needs* (DfEE 1997) and the Government strategy *Removing Barriers to Achievement* (DfES 2004). It should also be noted that there has been a growing recognition that in order for genuinely inclusive practice to become a reality the whole range of pupils' ability and needs must be recognised, assessed and addressed effectively. Thus expanding the notion of SEN to a much wider concept which recognises that all children, whatever their ability, should have the right to achieve their full educational potential within an inclusive mainstream educational setting.

This development in education is not, as mentioned earlier, confined to policy for education in England but can also be found in education policy throughout the world. Indeed in recent years there has been a plethora of initiatives and declarations from the United Nations concerning the right to an education for all and the rights of disabled persons to be included in education and society (1990, 1993, 1994, 2000, 2006). Perhaps one of the most influential of the initiatives in this area internationally, has been the 1994 Salamanca Statement (UNESCO) which can be seen to have influenced a great deal of thinking and policy making in the area of SEN and inclusion throughout the world. Here inclusion, the development of inclusive practice and the education of children with SEN in the mainstream of education as a means to ensuring equality of opportunity are endorsed and promoted in the following way:

We believe and proclaim that

every child has a fundamental right to education and must be given the opportunity to achieve and maintain an acceptable level of learning,

every child has unique characteristics, interests, abilities and learning needs, education systems should be designed and educational programmes implemented to take into account the wide diversity of these characteristics and needs, those with special educational needs must have access to regular schools which should accommodate them within a child centred pedagogy capable of meeting those needs,

regular schools with this inclusive orientation are the most effective means of combating discriminatory attitudes, creating welcoming communities, building an inclusive society and achieving education for all; moreover they provide an effective education to the majority of children and improve the efficiency and ultimately the cost-effectiveness of the entire education system
(Salamanca Statement 1994, pp viii–ix)

These principles, simply and clearly presented, were intended to inform and underpin a Framework for Action, which was agreed and endorsed by more than ninety countries throughout the world. The focus on education for all as a right, a child centred approach to pedagogy and the recognition and accommodation in schooling systems of individual differences, needs and interests seem, at face value, to be principles to which the majority of education professionals would sign up immediately. Perhaps more controversial and problematic in terms of policy, organisation and resourcing, however, was the notion that this education for all should take place in regular/mainstream schools with an inclusive orientation. More than seventeen years later, however, there is no doubt that this approach has influenced and continues to influence the development of policy, provision and indeed practice in education throughout the world, not only in the ninety plus countries which signed up initially to the Statement but also in many other countries. The fundamental right to an educational opportunity provided within the regular or mainstream school, for all children irrespective of their identified SEN, has led increasingly to education policy for integration and inclusion throughout the world.

In England, as in many developed countries of the world, alongside this more altruistic inspiration, policy has also been driven by economic concerns about the inexpediency of maintaining an expensive segregated system of provision alongside an increasingly expensive mainstream. This has resulted, in many cases, in the closure of segregated special schools and provision and the relocation of children with SEN and their support into the mainstream. Thus while the policy increasingly purports to be about *inclusion*, in reality it continues to be much more about the *integration* of organisation, provision and services for children with SEN into the mainstream of schooling often with little or no resultant change or modification to the mainstream itself. At the same time this process of *integration* has failed to a great extent to address, or to take account of, the exclusive subject oriented curriculum; the competitive assessment procedures; the lack of awareness and understanding of the needs of pupils with SEN and even in some cases the hostile attitudes which continue to be the status quo in the mainstream of education provision (Lloyd, 2008). This in turn has led to doubts about the potential for genuine participation for children with SEN in the mainstream and for its capacity to provide a genuinely equal educational opportunity for all children (Warnock, 2005). There is, as a result, genuine concern that policies for inclusion are not working and that children with SEN in the mainstream are not in fact experiencing genuine participation in education but are often experiencing exclusion within inclusion (Armstrong, Armstrong & Barton, 2000; Dyson, 2001; Benjamin, 2002; Warnock, 2005; Lloyd, 2008).

What has certainly become clear, as policy for inclusion has been developed and implemented, nationally and internationally, is that it is a difficult, problematic and contentious concept about which there is little or no consensus. Indeed it is possible to find numerous definitions in the wide range of literature on the subject, which is increasing daily (Dyson, 1999; Armstrong, Armstrong & Spandagou, 2010). Policy for inclusion continues, then, to be a contested, political, controversial, 'in your face' (Corbett & Slee, 2000) issue. A lack of conceptual clarity and agreement about what it means, however, creates not only the potential for confusion when it comes to further development of education policy but even greater problems for its implementation in practice where many interpretations can be found, which masquerade as inclusion or inclusive practice although they can be seen as having little to do with either.

The Impact of Policy for Inclusion on Practice

These policy changes and the imperative to move towards the inclusion of previously segregated groups of children with SEN into the mainstream of schooling have led, as mentioned above, to organisational changes and a wide range of new initiatives, in English schools. Further demands have arisen as a result of the growing recognition that the development of inclusion and inclusive practice impacts upon all pupils and their learning needs, irrespective of ability, and not just on those identified as having SEN. Some, though many would say insufficient, resourcing has been allocated, or reallocated, to support this process in the form of new funding mechanisms such as the Statementing Procedure. New support roles have emerged in the form of Special Education Needs Co-ordinators (SENCOs) and learning or classroom support staff. Many segregated special schools have been closed and where they remain open have been given new roles as resource centres or short stay units, in particular for those identified as having challenging behaviour.

While provision and support is now provided for the most part within the mainstream school/centre/classroom it also includes a variety of other forms and practices including units attached to or within mainstream schools; clusters and groups of schools which retain their original designation as special or ordinary schools but which are intended to work as consortia to promote inclusion; and even, what can be seen as a rather odd notion, segregated units within mainstream schools called inclusion units. A Code of Practice for SEN has been introduced (Department for Education and Science (DfES), 2001) which makes explicit the role of the mainstream teacher as responsible for the learning needs of all children and lays down more inclusive, collaborative procedures for identifying, addressing and monitoring children's SEN in the mainstream school with the Individual Education Plan (IEP) as a central tool to support these processes. The roles of the SENCO and learning support staff are also clarified, making clear that their job is the management of SEN in the school and to provide support to the teacher to enable him/her to support the child's learning. The role of parents as partners is increasingly seen as key to effective inclusion and the development of more inclusive approaches, as is multi professional/agency collaboration in the identification, assessment, monitoring and addressing of children's SEN and learning needs. All these changes have, of course, impacted considerably on the daily practice of teachers and indeed the whole range of education professionals and their development needs.

It is also important to recognise that during this same period, alongside policies for inclusion, a large number of other major education initiatives have been introduced in England, including the National Curriculum and associated testing regime; increased standardised, norm/age related assessment procedures; the inspection of schools tied to published league tables and of course the whole standards agenda which has dominated ITE and professional development. Throughout this period of rapid change there has been a failure to address, to recognise or take account of the fact that much of the education policy which has been introduced is in direct conflict with policy for inclusion, and indeed even has the potential to create barriers to genuine inclusion and to lead to greater exclusion (Barton & Armstrong 2007; Lloyd, 2008). Examples of this include the narrow subject oriented model underpinning the National Curriculum; the increasingly competitive nature of the standardised and norm related assessment procedures; the school effectiveness and standards agendas; the inspection regime and policies for the exclusion of pupils on grounds of challenging behaviour.

The tensions and pressures created by the amount and pace of change in education in England over a fairly short period of time, the demand for greater inclusion and the development of more inclusive practice can be seen, then, to have considerable implications for the development of the whole range of education professionals. For the majority, the implementation of these policies has led to a vast and increasing range of challenges including changes to their roles and responsibilities; new and increasing demands in terms of knowledge and understanding; increased pressure created by inspection and the need to meet a range of centrally determined professional standards; and the expectation that the learning of all children is the responsibility of the class/subject teacher, requiring awareness and understanding of the needs of pupils with SEN and how to identify and address them. Inevitably these demands have led, for many, to growing feelings of inadequacy to deal with the fast pace of change and the tensions created by conflicting policies and in some cases hostile attitudes towards change in the status quo of the mainstream of education provision (Lloyd, 2000; 2008). Armstrong, Armstrong and Spandagou (2010) cite teacher resistance to inclusion as a continuing critical factor and major barrier and refer to a teacher interviewed for a study in the USA following the implementation of the education policy for inclusion, *No Child Left Behind* (NCLB). This teacher expresses what she identifies as a commonly held view of education professionals, wrestling with the daily pressures they experience as a result of policy for inclusion, not just in the United States of America (USA), but also throughout the world.

> Teachers don't want them. If my job depends on their test scores and they are reading at first or second grade and I am teaching fourth grade...I don't want those kids. I do because I am a teacher and went into teaching to help kids. But if my job depends on it... I don't want those kids. (Harvey-Koelpin, 2006 p.140)

Given the issues discussed above it is no wonder, then, that despite the increasing demands of education policy to move toward inclusion, the development of genuinely inclusive practice in schools continues to be slow and patchy and that it is possible to identify a backlash against it.

> Although there has been a definite shift in attitude in recent years.... and a quite broad acceptance that children should not be segregated on the grounds of impairment, there is a counter-current moving against inclusive education which is gaining momentum. (Barton & Armstrong, 2007, p. 13)

This backlash, the barriers to developing genuinely inclusive practice in schools and the gap between the rhetoric of policy and the reality of practice are identified by a wide range of contributors to Barton and Armstrong's edited collection, *Policy, Experience and Change: Cross-Cultural Reflections on Inclusive Education* (op. cit.) from countries all over the world. Reasons cited are confused and contradictory policies; a lack of political will to enforce legislation; professional resistance to change; and in particular inadequate ITE and professional development.

> ...teachers are not confident about the adequacy of their professional preparation, special educator support, expertise and resources. Teachers require targeted training, classroom support and a school system that embraces inclusive education as excellent education for ALL. (Timmons, 2007, p.144).

One of the major implications of policy for inclusion is, then, that education professionals require more supportive, enabling and empowering ITE and professional development which identifies and addresses the issues and challenges facing them in their daily practice and equips them to develop positively, creatively and reflectively.

Issues for Practice Arising from Policy for Inclusion

A wider range of ability   The notion that the mainstream teacher is responsible for the learning needs of all children, together with the increased range of ability and diversity in the mainstream school arising from the implementation of policy for inclusion, are major issues. The expectation expressed in the policy (DfES, 2004) is that inclusion and the embedding of inclusive practice by teachers who are skilled and have the expertise necessary to identify, address and meet children's diverse needs are central to the achievement of the aims and intended outcomes of the strategy. As mentioned above, this raises a number of issues for ITE, professional development and support. Concerns have been expressed about whether children's learning needs are really being addressed effectively and whether they are experiencing greater access to genuine educational opportunity or not as a result of policy for inclusion. For example, in 2004 Ofsted identified that

> While most pupils with SEN are educated in mainstream schools progress towards inclusion in mainstream schools has slowed... Some pupils with SEN continue to face barriers to participation and achievement... Expectations for the success that pupils with SEN can have remains at the heart of the matter. Many of these could do better provided that the curriculum, learning and other support were better adapted to their needs and greater rigour was applied to setting and pursuing targets for achievement. (pp. 23–24)

The criticisms voiced within this statement point clearly to inadequate identification of pupils' learning needs. It also makes clear that together with high expectation of success, adequately addressing learning needs through rigorous targets is central to pupils' achievement. A major issue arising would therefore seem to be that education professionals and other involved agencies, need to be equipped, and need to work together, to identify the learning needs of the whole range of pupils effectively, irrespective of their ability. This process should be seen as the starting point for ensuring that pupils have access to an appropriate and challenging programme of study through which they will develop and achieve. The monitoring, and evaluation of the process of learning is also vitally important, of course, as is the production of appropriate evidence to demonstrate what learning has taken place.

Changing roles and responsibilities   Yet another issue for practice is the requirement for collaboration between the wide range of different professionals and agencies involved, which may include, amongst others, special and mainstream schools; SENCOs; learning/classroom support staff; specialist support staff and agencies; and teachers, pupils and parents. While there is no doubt that better communication and more joined up thinking are essential for the promotion of inclusion they are by no means easy to achieve. These groups have different, often competing, agendas and vested interests and can even regard each other as threats. While they may have the best interests of the child at the centre of their thinking they may also have conflicting opinions about how these interests may be best served and indeed about the value of inclusion itself to the child. Collaboration is difficult and requires the development of mutual respect, shared understanding and, most of all, time to develop (Keay & Lloyd, 2009). Much policy and strategy for inclusion, such as *Removing Barriers to Achievement* (DfES, 2004) depends on the development of just such collaboration and yet also fails to recognise that it cannot be achieved without considerable changes in practice. The implementation of any change inevitably meets with some resistance and the implementation of policy for inclusion requires a great deal of change. Changing, or changed, roles for teachers, other professionals, support staff, parents, pupils and for many others involved, without recognition that this may create tensions and problems, is doomed to failure. Parents are concerned to ensure that their children receive the best possible deal and will not be disadvantaged by the changes. Special education professionals and other professional groups are concerned that their expertise will be ignored or their jobs lost; and mainstream teachers held responsible, for the most part, for the implementation of a policy they do not fully understand, or in some cases even know about, feel inadequate and disempowered. The development of effective, sensitive and supportive inter professional and inter agency collaboration is, therefore, a key issue raised by the development of more inclusive practice.

Identifying, assessing and monitoring pupils' learning needs The exclusiveness and competitiveness of the mainstream schooling system with its norm related assessments, narrow content, subject based curriculum, age/stage related groupings has, as discussed earlier, remained largely unchanged and unchallenged by the implementation of policy for inclusion. The emphasis has been on a range of compensatory measures and learning support strategies to enable those children identified as having SEN to fit in, be normalised and achieve as best they can within the existing system. Achievement and success in the mainstream are measured, for the most part, against sets of predetermined, norm related standards through tests and examinations. Barton and Armstrong (2007) cite the Organisation for Economic Cooperation and Development (OECD) Programme for International Student Assessment (PISA) survey of 2003 as evidence of

> an increasing emphasis at the international level on student performance and measurement and of an obsession with 'standards'... The 'curriculum' has become increasingly controlled by the state in the interests of producing a labour force which will enhance productivity in the global market place. (p. 12)

For those children who fall behind or are unable to meet these standards, in spite of all their efforts and those of their support staff and teachers and parents, the experience inevitably leads to the reinforcement of failure. Benjamin (2002) sums this up, in relation to the English system where

> ...the standards agenda positions students to whom normative versions of success are not accessible as marginal, thus producing the conditions of exclusion within a system that claims to be moving towards inclusion. (p.136)

The issue of how children's learning needs are identified, addressed, monitored and evaluated is clearly then vitally important. The assessment of pupils' needs in genuinely inclusive practice is not about identifying or labelling them as having SEN, rather it should be flexible and sensitive. Formative assessment is necessary which begins with identifying what the child *can* do in order to build upon existing capability rather than a focus on what he/she *cannot* do in relation to sets of artificially created norms and standards. Ainscow (2003) makes the case that this sort of approach is central to inclusive practice and puts the focus on improving learning for all pupils not just those identified as having SEN.

This raises issues about individualising and personalising learning and indeed the whole approach to learning and teaching adopted, which are discussed in more detail in Chapter 6. It also reinforces the mandate of the Salamanca Statement (1994) that programmes of study should recognise children's unique, diverse abilities and characteristics and that their learning needs should be met through a child centred pedagogy which places the learner at the centre of the process.

Challenging Behaviour   Bagley (2007) makes the case that current pressures on teachers in English schools including class size and the demands of the standardised testing procedures are leading to increased exclusions of pupils particularly on grounds of challenging or inappropriate behaviour. Others have also raised concerns that policies for inclusion are not working and that many children in the mainstream continue to be excluded on grounds that their behaviour is unacceptable (Armstrong, Armstrong & Barton, 2000; Dyson, 2001; Benjamin, 2002; Warnock, 2005; Slee, 2007; Lloyd, 2008). Rustemier and Vaughan (2005), discussing the increasing numbers of children being excluded from the mainstream on grounds of behaviour, point to the subjective nature of judgements about behaviour and to the potential of the exclusivity and rigidity of the mainstream of education to create and exacerbate challenging and inappropriate behaviour. They raise issues about increasing pressure on education professionals and schools to conform to standards and meet targets leading to exclusions on grounds of behaviour. Clearly, then, the approach adopted for the assessment and management of behaviour, as either a tool for exclusion or as part of a policy for inclusion and the development of inclusive practice is another increasingly important issue.

CHAPTER 3

Initial training, initial teacher education and professional development needs   To
deal with the changes and challenges created by inclusion and the demand for more
inclusive practice, trainee and practising education professionals clearly need
access to supportive ITE or initial training and professional development, which
address the complex and problematic nature of inclusion and its implications. They
need to understand what inclusion is really about and to be able to critically reflect
on what it means for them personally and for their practice. They need access to
initial training and professional development, which will provide them with the
necessary understanding, skills and knowledge to meet the challenges discussed in
earlier sections of this chapter, which are many and vast. Booth, Nes and Stromstad
together with the other authors in their edited edition, *Developing Inclusive
Teacher Education* (2003), are, however, critical about the content and approach of
teacher education in relation to inclusion.

> The content of special needs teacher education is ambiguous about inclusion.
> Although inclusion is highlighted in many courses for teachers about special
> educational needs, it seems a deficit model still predominates. The mere
> existence of well-developed traditions of special needs education undermines
> calls for inclusion and the school for all, signalling that some children are
> 'other' and not the responsibility of the general teacher. (p. 172)

ITE is seen as being far too subject and content focussed with the issue of inclusion
and inclusive education focussing on SEN and excluded groups rather than being
treated as a philosophy underpinning the whole approach to education about
education for all, participation and equity. For Slee (2007) this approach is about
inclusive education being seen as an "add-on" or the "repackaging of special
education" (p.184).

In much the same way a great deal of professional development in the area tends
to focus on specialised courses, or modules within programmes of study, dealing
with topics like autism, dyslexia, behaviour management. While such professional
development may appear to address the day-to-day needs of education
professionals in terms of providing a quick fix solution it does not assist with the
project of developing genuine inclusion and rather can be seen to support and
ensure the continuation of the status quo. This sort of professional development
fails to address the very serious and urgent challenges discussed earlier in this
chapter such as dealing with the fast pace of change; developing effective inter
professional/agency collaboration; and working with parents; ensuring full
participation for all pupils irrespective of ability. In addition to these issues, as
discussed in Chapter 6, for education professionals in England additional pressure
has been added in the area of professional development by demands for education
professionals to demonstrate evidence of the impact of their professional
development on pupils' learning. While this can be seen to be a laudable and
valuable accountability strategy in terms of public spending and indeed also from
an educational perspective legitimate, there is no doubt that in practice it creates

further dilemmas and has become and continues to be an important and problematic issue.

Some Positive Strategies for Practice

Having raised and discussed some of the problematic issues facing education professionals, arising from the implementation of policy for inclusion it is important to focus, in conclusion, on some positive strategies which might assist and support them. Ainscow, in an interview with Corbett and Slee (2000) makes clear the importance, for the development of inclusion and inclusive practice, of education professionals and practitioners engaging with a process of continuous critical enquiry into their own practice. Indeed for him

> Inclusive education is really a process of people enquiring into their own context to see how it can be developed and it is a process of growth. It is a social process and it engages people in making sense of their experience and helping one another to question their experience and their context to see how things can be moved on. (Mel Ainscow, interviewed 26th October 1998)

Looking back to the principles that underpinned the Salamanca Statement (1994), it seems that they have the potential to provide an excellent starting point for such a process of enquiry. The voice of students and pupils is also an important starting point for reflecting on and better understanding inclusion and inclusive practice. The list below, provided by children from all sectors of schooling and published in the Guardian Newspaper (June 5th, 2001), describes the school that they would like and provides an excellent, inclusive, framework in which to critically examine the learning and teaching context.

A beautiful school with glass dome roofs to let in the light, uncluttered classrooms and brightly coloured walls.

A comfortable school with sofas and beanbags, cushions on the floors, tables that don't scrape our knees, blinds that keep out the sun, and quiet rooms where we can chill out.

A safe school with swipe cards for the school gates, anti-bully alarms, first aid classes and someone to talk to about our problems.

A listening school with children on the governing body, class representatives and the chance to vote for the teachers.

A flexible school without rigid timetables or exams, without compulsory homework, without a one size fits all curriculum, so we can follow our own interests and spend more time on what we enjoy.

A relevant school where we learn through experience, experiments and exploration, with trips to historic sites and teachers who have practical experience of what they teach.

A respectful school where we are not treated as empty vessels to be filled with information, where teachers treat us as individuals, where children and adults can talk freely to each other, and our opinion matters.

A school without walls so we can go outside to learn, with animals to look after and wild gardens to explore

A school for everybody with boys and girls from all backgrounds and abilities, with no grading, so we don't compete against each other but just do our best.

Certainly schools and education practice informed and underpinned by these principles would inevitably be more inclusive and would have the potential to provide more genuine access to learning and participation for *all* children. Inclusive practice, informed by principles which promote full participation in education as a right for all, addresses the individual learning needs of every child through a learner/child centred pedagogy and recognises individual differences interests and abilities, has the potential to improve all teaching and thus the learning experience of all children.

The process of coming to a clearer understanding about the implications of inclusion and the development of inclusive practice cannot, however, be achieved in a vacuum and it is important to think about how it might be facilitated in practice and how education professionals might be encouraged and supported to take responsibility for, and engage with the project. The following four inextricably linked areas, which are recurrent themes in the discussion throughout this book and which underpin the approach to professionalism and practice which we believe to be essential for the model of professional development we propose to work effectively, should therefore be addressed.

ITE and professional development The importance of access for education professionals to enabling and empowering ITE and professional development is crucial in order to raise awareness about inclusion and inclusive practice. ITE and professional development should focus on the development of knowledge and understanding and provide support and develop actively engaged professionals who welcome challenge, are equipped for change and seek to constantly develop themselves and their practice. This approach is discussed more fully in Chapter 2.

Critically reflective practice The development, through such ITE and professional development, of an approach where education professionals expect, and have the necessary skills, abilities and opportunities, to engage, continuously, in a process of critical reflection on, and evaluation of, their practice with a view to identifying areas for change and development, is also vitally important to facilitate the development of inclusive practice.

Professionally orientated research It is also essential, as discussed in Chapter 2, for the development of such critically reflective practice that education professionals learn how to engage actively in rigorous, systematic professionally oriented research which is designed to address important problems and issues and to produce real evidence which can be used to inform ideas about the meaning of inclusion and inclusive practice and to empower professionals in the field. In a paper given at a conference in 2005, Stephen Kemmis made a strong case for high quality critical practitioner research to 'address important problems in thought and action, in theory and practice for the good of education, for the good of each person and for the good of our societies.' (p 18). For him, practitioners who engage with research that meets these criteria have the potential to transform and reform practice

> They will engage themselves in communicative action to inform themselves about the perennial question 'what is to be done?' And their answers will be in the form of transformed practice, transformed practitioners, and transformed settings in which their practice occurs. (ibid)

Collaboration As discussed earlier, these approaches are strengthened and supported through collaborative endeavour. There is also a vitally important need to develop genuine collaboration between the many different agencies involved in inclusion and the development of inclusive practice. Again ITE and professional development have an important role to play in raising awareness and developing the necessary skills understanding and attitudes that education professionals need in order to collaborate effectively. However, perhaps the best way to learn about collaboration is by collaborating. Engaging with practical projects and/or the type of critical action research projects mentioned above, which involve a range of different groups and interests and where there is an opportunity to learn from and with each other, can assist with developing more genuine collaborative and inclusive and approaches which will support inclusion and strengthen inclusive practice. Again, Stephen Kemmis makes the case that this sort of collaborative action is essential if we are really going to ensure that genuine change and development take place in education

> Community education, community action and community participation is needed – perhaps through critical action research projects that can bring people together around major issues and themes requiring shared deliberation about our shared fate and future. (ibid p. 17)

Clearly it is not sufficient to address these areas alone but they do provide some starting points. They also point clearly to the importance for education professionals of access to, and participation in, a process of professional education and development, which enables them to empower themselves to address the challenges of inclusion for their own learning and that of their pupils.

CHAPTER SUMMARY

The aim of this chapter has been to identify and come to a clearer understanding about some of the factors influencing what can be seen as the gap between policy for, and practice in, inclusive education. Perhaps the most important issue arising from this brief investigation can be seen as the need for education professionals from all areas of practice to engage with each other in a process of reaching a better, and hopefully, shared understanding of what inclusion is about and what this means in terms of its impact on, and implications for, their practice. This process requires that education professionals have access to and engage with empowering initial training, ITE and professional development, which provides them with the understanding, skills and abilities to engage in, reflect on, debate and research their practice collaboratively and which recognises and welcomes the controversial, political, contentious nature of these activities.

SECTION 2

MEASURING IMPACT

HIGH QUALITY PROFESSIONAL
DEVELOPMENT

There is a great deal of consensus amongst policy makers, education researchers and education professionals about the importance of high quality professional development and its link to improving and developing practice in education. However there is less agreement about what constitutes high quality in professional development and about how it can be distinguished given the wide range and variety of provision available, and of providers. Addressing this theme, Armour (2006) makes the case that the quality of professional development opportunities for teachers, and we would suggest all education professionals, is an issue of increasing concern. "Concerns about the nature and quality of teachers' continuing professional development (CPD) are shared around the world and across curriculum subjects." (p. 203). She supports her view with reference to Borko's description of the professional development opportunities available to teachers as 'woefully inadequate' (2004, p.3).

The perspective, that the quality of professional development in education is an issue of increasing concern which requires urgent attention, is also endorsed and supported further afield, for example in the United States' National Staff Development Council (NSDC) report, *Professional Learning in the Learning Professions* (Darling-Hammond et al., 2009), which makes clear its value and importance.

"Educators and policymakers increasingly recognize the importance of providing high quality learning opportunities to help transform teaching." (p. 7). The report goes on, in a review of international and national research in the area, to identify that while there is a clear need for intensive, sustained, supportive high quality professional development there are major concerns that a majority of American teachers (59%) are negative about the value of many of the professional development opportunities available to them. These concerns, being expressed nationally and internationally, inevitably raise questions about what can be seen as relevant and apposite professional development and about how its quality is assured and monitored.

Building upon the analysis of professionalism provided in Chapter 2, this chapter explores issues relating to the quality assurance of professional development opportunities. It draws on research, carried out with a wide range and variety of professional development providers, which examined the implementation of a self-regulated model of quality assurance designed to address some of the concerns raised above about the relevance and quality of professional development. Links between different forms of professionalism and the quality assurance of professional development opportunities are also examined in relation to the research and readers will be challenged to consider the role of a professional community in ensuring high quality learning opportunities.

QUALITY ASSURANCE AND PROFESSIONAL DEVELOPMENT

For some time now, education in England has been subjected to the scrutiny, inspection and audit of independent external agencies, such as the Office for Standards in Education (Ofsted) and the Quality Assurance Agency (QAA), as part of a move by succeeding governments to increase accountability and demonstrate improvement and effectiveness. This development has been linked to the imposition of a plethora of standards against which education professionals and the institutions in which they work, including early childhood centres, schools, colleges and universities, are measured and held publicly accountable (www.tda.gov.uk/ teachers/continuingprofessionaldevelopment). Blackmore (2004) points out that the standards focussed approach to inspection and audit was originally intended for the manufacturing market, and is an approach that has more to do with quality control and compliance than quality assurance and enhancement. On the same theme, Alderman and Brown (2005) raise the question 'Can Quality Assurance Survive the Market?' In a discussion comparing procedures for audit in higher education in the UK and the USA, they are critical about the dominant approach that has been developed in response to increased market pressures.

> There are those, including the present authors, who feel that audit has already moved… in the direction of a 'tick box' approach as audit teams struggle to monitor compliance with a raft of externally (i.e. Government) imposed items such as institutional information about quality. (p.323)

Critics have pointed out that the imposition of this sort of model of external quality control on education has led to education professionals feeling marginalised, leading them to regard themselves as passive victims of inspection and audit, rather than active participants in a developmental process of quality assurance (MacBeath, 1999; Burns, 2005; Chapman, 2004: Keay & Lloyd, 2009).

More recently, changes have been made to the Ofsted and QAA inspection and review procedures, which place more emphasis on self-evaluation and require more active engagement by professionals, suggesting some recognition of the criticisms above. These changes require an approach to inspection and audit, "…that views quality assurance as a professional attitude of mind, embedded deeply in the individual academic and institutional consciousness rather than as a response to demands for bureaucratic procedures and compliance" (Willams, 2007, p.1). Such an approach inevitably places responsibility on education professionals themselves to be actively involved in the processes of enhancing and ensuring the quality of their provision with a view to developing and improving it and requires adopting a positive attitude towards quality assurance as an integral part of their professional practice. In spite of these changes, promoted as developmental and concerned with quality enhancement rather than quality control and quality processes rather than outcomes, education professionals remain sceptical about their role and involvement in quality assurance procedures. In earlier work (Keay & Lloyd, 2009), we identify that:

> What is clear is that while a great deal of theorising and critique has taken place about the role of QA *(quality assurance)* agencies and the way the processes of inspection have impacted on education and practice, little of it seems to have affected the way in which professionals themselves see their own role in these processes. In the main they adopt a passive reactive role to QA, accepting that it is a requirement and not something they would consider initiating for the development of good practice. (p. 658)

These conclusions, drawn as a result of research carried out with a wide range of providers of professional development, which will be discussed later in this chapter, impacted considerably on the development of the process model presented in this book. This model is intended to support and encourage education professionals to engage in a process of development, change and improvement in education, seen as a "... continuous process of engagement and an expectation of professionalism and professionals by professionals." (ibid). As a result of engaging in this continuous process, one of the intended outcomes is that education professionals will be more motivated and will become more active participants in assessing, monitoring and evaluating the quality and relevance of the professional development which they access. This in turn should enable them, and through their feedback professional development providers, to articulate more clearly what constitutes high quality professional development and the criteria by which it can, and should, be measured.

Linking Professional Development to Development and Improvement in Education

In addition to the developments and changes in quality assurance procedures relating to professional development for education professionals, over the past twenty years or so, in England, there has also been a move, seen by many as part of the wider strategy by government to marketise education (Ball, 1990 Gerwitz, 2002), to establish funding systems for professional development which depend on an open bidding process. This has encouraged independent providers and businesses to bid alongside the more traditional professional development providers such as Local Authorities (LAs) and HEIs, and has inevitably led to concerns about how the quality of both provision and providers can be monitored and assured. As a further extension of this, and in a move to demonstrate better value for money in education, much funding available for professional development has also been tied to the implementation of the vast array of government initiatives resulting in the one size fits all sort of professional development provision, designed to support their implementation, which is often offered off site in the form of short courses or one-off events. Accountability, inspection and audit processes for funding allocated through bidding processes require that evidence of impact on pupils' learning and school improvement and effectiveness is demonstrated, a problematic issue discussed in more detail below and further in Chapter 6.

Yet another aspect of the changes to funding, which can be seen as problematic, is the direct allocation of funds to access professional development to schools and institutions. This has been done with the intention of forging and further reinforcing the direct link between professional development and pupil achievement, school/institution improvement and effectiveness and to performance. The TDA *Strategy for the professional development of the children's workforce* (2009) makes this clear:

> Effective PD (*professional development*) is not an end in itself, it is integral to the effectiveness of the school and to improving the achievement and wellbeing of children and young people. By linking professional development with school improvement planning, performance review processes, professional standards and individuals planning their own professional development there is a proven process which is used by the best schools to support successful and sustainable school improvement. (p.9)

As Armour (2006) points out, however, while there can be seen to be considerable consensus in research and literature that effective professional development does indeed have the potential to impact on pupils' learning and achievement and on school improvement, it is a complex and problematic process. Questions arise about the characteristics of effective professional development and about how evidence of impact on improvement can be measured and demonstrated. Notwithstanding these issue and problems, it is also important to point out that school improvement and effectiveness can be seen to be different and, by some, as contentious issues and their direct link to professional development therefore controversial.

Field (2005), looking at professional development as a means to school development, provides useful, distinctions between school effectiveness, school improvement and school transformation. The table below takes this distinction further to examine the relationship between school targets, professional development and professionalism.

Table 2. The relationship between school targets and professional development

	Aim	*Measured by*	*Professional development focus*	*Mode of development*	*Professionalism*
School effectiveness	Raising standards	Compliance Imposed targets	Institutional needs	School-based for whole institution	Managerial
School improvement	Capacity building and empowerment	Individual and institutional targets self imposed targets	Individual and institutional needs	Critically reflective practice	Democratic
School transformation	Changing and reforming practices	Individual and institutional targets self imposed targets	Individual and institutional needs	Critically reflective practice	Democratic

School effectiveness is concerned with raising standards and is linked closely to, and measured by, compliance with government imposed performance related targets and criteria. Professional development to support it is linked, therefore, to performance management, departmental and school plans and needs and priorities are identified in terms of measurable performance targets with an emphasis on the institutional needs and requirements. Professional development provision, as a result, is often school based with the needs of the whole institution rather than the individual used as the criterion for relevance. In terms of models of professionalism, discussed in Chapter 2, school effectiveness can be seen to be closely connected with managerial models. School improvement is concerned with capacity building and empowerment and relies on a supportive enabling culture, which recognises individual as well as institutional needs. School transformation, as it suggests, is about changing practices for the better. Professional development to support processes of improvement and transformation is geared towards the development of critical, reflective, analytical, evaluative skills and to creative forward planning and recognises that addressing the developmental professional needs of individuals is key to institutional change and reform. The latter two processes can be seen, therefore, to be associated with *democratic* models of professionalism. It is clear from this, albeit extremely brief, analysis and from the discussion about models of professionalism in Chapter 2, that the purpose, role and provision of professional development to support and achieve the desired aims and outcomes of each process is inevitably going to be very different (Kennedy, 2005). In the same way, measures and evidence of the effectiveness and quality of professional development will, of necessity, differ according to which of these processes is deemed desirable as an outcome.

The government *Strategy for the professional development of the children's workforce* (TDA, 2009), however, links all three processes as desirable and indeed inevitable outcomes of effective professional development. In doing so it conflates all three, using the language of effectiveness, improvement and transformation interchangeably, as evidenced in the quotation cited above. While it recognises the need for a variety of professional development options these are all discussed in relation to school plans, national standards, performance management, targets and outcomes and can therefore be seen to be more associated with effectiveness than with improvement or transformation. This can be seen as unhelpful and confusing and as contributing further complexity to the issue of identifying the characteristics of high quality, appropriate and relevant professional development. The impact of professional development measured in terms of performance in relation to government/school plans and targets can also be seen to require a very different set of evidence from impact measured in terms of capacity building and empowerment of staff and students. Similarly, as discussed further in Chapter 6, concepts of achievement and what counts as evidence of pupils' success are also open to debate and discussion and differ according to the stance adopted, making simplistic links to the impact of professional development potentially dangerous and confusing.

The discussion above is intended to highlight some of the problems and difficulties facing education professionals in relation to the professional development they want and need to access and providers of professional development in relation to the purpose and role of their provision and to both groups in terms of ensuring the quality of professional development. Armour (2006) summarises some of the tensions experienced by education professionals as a result of some of the issues and problems discussed above;

> …they are exasperated by CPD that is offered out of context and that cannot be transferred to their schools; they want to focus closely on the specific needs of their pupils; they value learning with and from colleagues and want more opportunities to learn in this way; and they will even tolerate 'official' CPD simply for the chance it offers to learn informally with professional colleagues. (p. 204)

Burns (2005) also refers to the "struggle between school needs and individual needs" experienced by education professionals where "the schools' needs had to take precedence" (p. 361) as a result of the pressures of external inspection requirements and the needs to meet targets. School based funding available for professional development is also seen as strongly influencing the drive for institutional needs to take priority over individual staff development needs. These factors have led, according to Burns, to

– a mismatch between perceptions of what is and should be the focus of professional CPD;

- dominance of management control;
- the influence of the School Development Plan (SDP) and performance management on CPD for individuals;
- teachers' identification with the schools' needs as their own professional needs. (p. 359)

This, in turn, has led to a lack of professional autonomy and, of more concern, to a lack of motivation and opportunity for teachers to think about, and address their professional development needs in a structured way.

> If the current managerial education context and accountability encourage teachers to take on the role of compliant employee... this has wider implications. It points to the need to consider the effect on teachers' beliefs about themselves and their professional learning within such a system of required competencies and inspections. (op cit, p. 367)

It would seem from these concerns that education professionals would welcome, and indeed are in need of, access to a range of professional development provision which enables them to balance their own professional development needs against those of the institutions in which they work and the demands of government initiatives and focuses on supporting them to meet the learning needs of their pupils and students. This view was endorsed strongly by participants at a symposium on professional development, organised by the Guardian Newspaper together with the TDA (16th June 2009). Good professional development for the whole children's workforce was seen as crucial for meeting children's learning needs but current provision was criticised for being too government initiative and school focused with the danger that 'the weakest schools can become more vulnerable' and leads to provision where 'we are getting one size fits all'. Summarising, the article reports, "CPD, it was concluded, works best where the individual, the system and the school join together to meet the needs of the child." This issue is discussed in more detail in Chapter 5 where control of professional development is considered.

There is a clear recognition by professionals, in government policy and in research and literature, in the area, that effective professional development has an important role to play in the improvement and development of practice in education and further analysis of effective professional development is presented in Chapter 5. What is also clear, however, from the issues raised above is that provision of, and access to, appropriate and relevant professional development is problematic and complex. What constitutes appropriate and relevant professional development depends upon the intended aims and outcomes and demands of individual professionals and the institutions in which they work and indeed government targets and objectives, which may well be in conflict. Questions about the quality of professional development provision are, similarly, determined and raised in relation to this range of potentially conflicting demands. A major issue of concern in terms of quality assurance, whatever the aims or intended outcomes of the professional development for the individual or institution, is however its impact on professional practice, on the institution and most importantly on the pupils/students and their learning. There is no doubt that impact and demonstrating evidence of impact have become increasingly important measures of quality in the area and are of considerable concern to education professionals.

Characteristics of High Quality Professional Development

Ingvarson et al., (2005), in a discussion about factors influencing the impact of professional development programmes on knowledge and practice, which draws on studies done as part of the Australian Government Quality Teacher Programme, identify a number of characteristics which were associated in the studies with high quality, effective professional development. These include a focus on what the pupil/students are to learn and how to deal with any problems they may face with the learning; research based knowledge about students' learning in the area and opportunities to examine, and reflect on students' work together with colleagues.

> They led teachers to actively reflect on their practice and to compare it with high standards for professional practice. They engage them in identifying what they needed to learn, and in planning the learning experiences that would help them meet those needs. They provided time for teachers to test new teaching methods and to receive follow-up support and coaching in their classrooms as they faced problems of implementing changes. They included activities that led teachers to deprivatise their practice and gain feedback about their teaching from colleagues. (p. 16)

These findings are reinforced by those of Darling-Hammond et al., (2009) who identify, in a study of international research in the area, four principles for effective professional development, which should

– be intensive, ongoing and connected to practice;
– focus on student learning and address the teaching of specific curriculum content;
– align with school improvement priorities and goals;
– build strong working relationships among teachers.

These principles are echoed by Desimone (2009) in her attempt to identify a core conceptual framework through which to study and critically examine professional development where she identifies a set of critical features, which define effective professional development, content focus, active learning, coherence, duration and collective participation. Clearly it is possible to identify common themes across the work of these authors and that of others in the field (Day & Qing Gu, 2010; Eraut, 1994) and it is also reflected in government strategy (TDA, 2009), which identifies three priorities for effective professional development; to embed a learning culture; to increase coherence and collaboration; and to improve quality and capacity.

In addition to these characteristics there is a clear emphasis in the research and literature in the area on the importance of impact and the ability to demonstrate evidence of impact on practice and in particular on the learning of students/pupils as a result of effective professional development. Guskey (in Kreider & Bouffard, 2006), discussing his five level model for evaluating professional development makes clear the importance of evidence in evaluating the impact of professional development but also points to the problematic nature of what constitutes valid evidence. His findings point to the need for a variety of different types of evidence and for a range of different stakeholders to be involved from the onset in decisions about what evidence should be collected in order to demonstrate successful impact. He also identifies the need for education professionals, who are trying out new strategies as a result of professional development, to plan for the ongoing collection of evidence as an in-built feature of the implementation since continuous feedback is necessary to demonstrate that while the strategy might not yield results for a period of time it can nevertheless be seen to be making a difference. These issues are addressed in more detail in Chapter 6 and Guskey's model is discussed further in relation to the development of the model presented in this book in Chapter 7.

From the very brief discussion above we believe that it is possible to identify some essential ingredients, which can be seen to be indicators of high quality professional development for education professionals. These include, in no particular order, as they are all equally essential:

- the active engagement and involvement of professionals in the identification of their own professional development needs;
- professional development which is informed by and supports professionals to identify and address their pupils'/students' learning needs;
- professional development which is geared towards improving, developing and transforming professional practice;
- professional development which engages professionals in a process of learning at their own level as well as about their pupils'/students' learning;
- support to implement new strategies and to critically evaluate and reflect on their success in collaboration with colleagues;
- a research approach which supports the identification, collection and evaluation of evidence of impact of the strategies employed as a result of the professional development on their practice and on their pupils'/students' learning;
- professional development which is underpinned by and supports the development of a collaborative community of practice.

This is not, of course, an exhaustive list but it provides some of the key starting points which underpinned the development of the model presented in this book which was also inspired by the findings of research, commissioned by the Professional Development Board-Physical Education, UK (PDB-PE) to evaluate the implementation, and contribute to, the development of an evidence based, developmental, self regulated process of quality assurance for professional development providers in the subject area (Keay & Lloyd, 2009; Keay & Lloyd, 2008a).

Research Into Quality Standards in Professional Development – A Case Study

The PDB-PE was established in 2001 by the DfEE with the task, as with other similar associations in other curriculum subject areas, to monitor and enhance quality of professional development provision (Whitehead, 2004). Processes of application for Kite Marking, or to be a Licensed Provider, were initially devised by the PDB-PE but at the time the research was commissioned were attracting few applications. The research was intended to evaluate these processes together with a wide range and variety of professional development providers, some of whom had applied for a Kite Mark or Licence and some who had not, and to test out categories of quality standards to see if they were considered relevant and appropriate indicators of quality. The aim was to provide feedback, which would assist in the development of a "more user-friendly, accessible, evidence based system of quality assurance and enhancement" (Keay & Lloyd, 2009, p. 661). Longitudinal research, was carried out in three stages and involved a wide range of professional development providers working in the area of physical education and school sport including, HEIs, LAs, schools and colleges, private businesses and national government organisations and bodies from all over England and involved a range of data gathering techniques. The three stages comprised:

– Evaluation, through document research and interviews, of the existing system of Kite Marking and Licensing and discussion and evaluation of the categories of quality standards identified by the PDB-PE against which quality professional development provision should be measured.
– Evaluation of a revised, single process of application for PDB-PE approval using a modified process of self evaluation against the categories of quality standards agreed as an outcome of Stage 1.
– The collation of case study material, together with providers, which had achieved approval through the new revised application process, which could be used to demonstrate *good* practice.

Full details of the research and discussion about the findings, which were submitted to the PDB-PE in 2005, have been written up elsewhere (Keay & Lloyd, 2008a). Some important themes emerged from the findings of the research, however, which, as stated above, inform and underpin the discussion in this chapter about high quality professional development and its quality assurance. The findings from Stage 1 of the research were that providers welcomed a developmental process of quality assurance and that they felt strongly that the process should impact on their practice and assist them to improve and develop it. Engaging in such a process was seen as a good, awareness raising activity, as was the intention to produce examples of *good* practice as case studies and to share and disseminate them. The notion of a buddy system was also suggested which could support, enable and facilitate this process of sharing *good* practice between providers. Another clear theme was that impact of provision should be more clearly linked to children's learning. These recommendations and findings were fed back to the PDB-PE and informed the revision of a new, single, process of application for approval, which invited providers to assess and evaluate their provision against a set of quality standards in order to obtain recognition of quality by the PDB-PE, a process subject to regular review. During Stage 2 of the research, which evaluated the newly implemented procedure of application with a wide range and variety of providers who had, and also some who had not, applied for PDB-PE recognition, far richer and more informative data was collected. Providers were enthusiastic about the process as an awareness raising developmental tool, as in Stage 1, but found it to be time consuming. Where it had been used there was consensus that it had provided useful feedback, which had contributed to improving practice, and had also highlighted important areas of quality assurance that could and should be improved. Where it had not been used providers cited confusion about the role of the PDB-PE, if they had even heard of it, and although they felt recognition was important and might improve their practice and provision felt that they needed assistance with the process of application.

Perhaps more importantly for the discussion above about high quality professional development, providers were, for the most part, insecure about how they could demonstrate evidence of impact of their provision on practice and especially on the learning of the end users of the provision, the pupils and students. They were also extremely confused about what counts as evidence of impact and felt that they needed help and support in this area. For the most part evidence cited consisted of tick sheets and evaluation forms filled in by participants at the end of professional development sessions and, even when follow up sessions took place at a later date with participants to discuss impact, the evidence was mostly concerned with the practice and learning of the participants rather than the learning of their pupils/students. A common theme was the view of the majority of providers that the development of a community of practice would provide excellent networking possibilities, provide support and create opportunities for sharing and developing practice and addressing some of the problems arising with regard to impact and evidence, which were not always available. This view was reinforced during Stage 3 of the research during which the examples of 'good' practice were gathered and disseminated as case studies.

The findings of this research, clearly, support the points made above about the complexity and problematic nature of identifying and assuring high quality professional development. Particular issues which arise, are the importance of active engagement by professionals in the processes of quality assurance in order to raise awareness and impact on practice. In addition, education professionals are insecure and lack confidence about the whole issue of what counts as evidence of impact on practice, especially when it comes to evidence of impact on the learning of pupils/students. A third important issue is the importance and value of developing a collaborative community of practice or professional learning community.

CHAPTER 4

Professional Learning Communities

The importance of developing professional learning communities as a key strategy for improving, changing and developing practice in education, as discussed in Chapter 3, is recognised in much of the research and literature about professional development (Bolam et al., 2005). Such a community can also be seen as key to developing and ensuring the quality of provision. Certainly in the research described above the majority of professional development providers were clear that the development of networking possibilities to exchange and disseminate *good* practice, and to work together to address some of the problems and issues they faced, was an important support for learning about quality and quality assurance and one to which they would eagerly subscribe. Indeed, it can be seen as having an essential role to play in the development of self regulated quality assurance procedures and was a clear recommendation resulting from the research. Burns (2005) sees the development of a professional learning community as an important strategy for combating some of the problems raised earlier in this chapter about the increasing focus of professional development on effectiveness, external targets, and prioritisation of government initiatives over individual professional capacity building and learning. It also has great potential in combating alienation, isolation and impoverished learning opportunities, which education professionals can experience as a result of the increasing drive towards institution-based professional development.

> Studies in schools found that the norm of teaching had been isolation and independent practice and it is rare to have the time to develop networks for support and professional learning. In collaborative learning cultures innovation flourished and teacher isolation was significantly reduced. (Anderson, 2002, p. 20)

However, it is also important to note Burns' (2005) reference to the work of Mitchell and Sackney (2000) who stress that learning communities may contribute to, but are not synonymous with, the notion of learning organisations which are

> .... dedicated to organisational effectiveness and efficiency. The ends are goals set by the gatekeepers, and the means to these ends are the people - the teachers. In contrast, in learning communities, they suggest that the ends are the growth and development of the members of the community. (p. 369)

The idea of learning organisations can be seen to fit more closely with a managerial model of professionalism rather than a democratic model, which indeed depends on strategies such as the establishment of a collaborative or professional learning community for its development, an issue which is discussed in more detail in Chapter 7. Anderson (2002), in work done in New Zealand to foster and embed collaborative learning cultures in schools concludes that it is not an easy process to build and sustain them. She stresses that their development requires time and that participants need to feel that there is something in it for them. They need to feel that they are learning something new and/or useful, but they also need to feel that they have something to contribute which is valued by the other members if they are to engage fully with the process. The outcome is, however, well worth the effort.

Elliott (2007) proposes the development of a "networked professional learning community" (p. 240) as a key strategy for the development and assessment of the quality of practitioner research which is, as discussed in Chapter 3, an important component of high quality professional development. He proposes criteria against which the quality of collaborative action research should be measured, which would seem to be equally useful indicators of high quality for professional development, which has the potential to foster the development of, and to support, a professional learning community. It should:

– Exemplify a democratic process – where actions are held up to the scrutiny of professional peers and modification is a potential outcome of this process;
– Foster the development of experimental work across the network;
– Assist with the identification of discernable features which are practically relevant;
– Enable the collective construction of knowledge;
– Enable shared understanding;
– Make a significant contribution to the development of understanding theory;
– Enable the systematic presentation of shared understanding and insights in a publicly accessible form.

A professional learning community dedicated to meeting these criteria for quality is, we believe, a vitally important component in the development of a model of self-initiated, self regulated quality assurance for professional development, of the sort being developed by the PDB-PE and described above. By adopting this proactive approach to quality assurance, education professionals have the potential to engage with, and take increasing responsibility for, development, improvement and transformation of themselves and their practice in education.

CHAPTER SUMMARY

This chapter has discussed different approaches employed to assure the quality of education in England and further afield with a particular focus on professional development provision. The case is made that high quality professional development in education requires that education professionals are motivated to engage actively and collaboratively in a process of self initiated quality assurance in order to ensure that the provision available to them is appropriate, relevant and meets their individual needs and the learning needs of their pupils/students as well as those of the institutions in which they work. Findings from research in the area with professional development providers set up to evaluate a self regulatory process of quality assurance have been used to illustrate the value of such a process and the importance of developing professional learning communities for the development and success of the approach.

CHAPTER 5

IMPACT OF PROFESSIONAL DEVELOPMENT

Impact driven professional development can lead to a narrow learning experience for education professionals and for children, if implemented carefully, however, it has the potential to lead to an inclusive approach to teaching and learning that works towards ensuring that every child's learning needs are addressed. This inclusive approach to practice in education underpins and is key to the success of the model presented in this book, as discussed in more detail in Chapter 3. Current literature and research on the impact of professional development, however, highlights the difficulties we face in ensuring that professional development has an impact on young people's learning and raises many questions about how we can improve the educational experience of young people through the professional development of the education workforce. One of the ways in which we can improve their experiences is to ensure that professional learning has a measurable impact and this chapter and Chapter 6 examine what this means for education professionals and their pupils. This chapter explores the current political and economic climate in which interest in impact is visible in every area of education, highlighting the positive outcomes and also the dangers. It raises questions about the control of professional development and examines previous research to ask why we should measure impact and how this links to effective professional development.

MEASURING IMPACT

The issue of measuring impact and providing evidence of the effectiveness of educational activity is currently, as mentioned above, of great political and economic interest. For some time schools in the state sector in England have had to provide evidence of the effect of education provision on pupils. However, the requirement to measure impact takes this a stage further across a range of education activity, for example, the new format of the Research Excellence Framework in the UK, which will assess the quality of research undertaken by university staff now requires evidence of the impact of research. There is not only concern relating to value for the money invested in research, but there is also interest in the effectiveness and influence of the research conducted in higher education. Another example of this may be found in a national post-graduate professional development programme in England, which requires evidence of impact as a criterion for award and continued funding by the Government, an issue which will be discussed in more detail later in this chapter. Other examples of concern about, and interest in, impact include large-scale surveys undertaken by the Government to assess the effectiveness of education, for example the Newly

Qualified Teacher Survey and the National Student Survey. Results from both surveys are published nationally and used by the media, independent analysts and Government agencies to assess the impact of provision. The language used in education is also symbolic of the interest in impact; evidence, performance (management), inspection, review and audit have all become familiar elements of the policy language and rhetoric used to examine effectiveness.

Value for Money and Accountability

Policy interest in impact appears to have two driving forces, which, while they can be examined separately, are also closely related, they are value for money and accountability. In relation to 'value for money' the current economic climate is clearly highly influential and while this is of relatively recent political and policy interest in relation to professional development, it is feasible to assume that it will remain of concern for the foreseeable future. However, as discussed later in this chapter, in a section on the control of professional development, the issue of accountability has been with us, and has been growing in momentum, for several decades. Apple (2009) identifies a combination of three elements of influence, which can be seen to affect the way education is funded, provided and evaluated, which are useful in examining current imperatives around impact. Firstly, he identifies neo-liberals, who believe that private is necessarily good and public necessarily bad, as influential in the changing scenario of the management and funding of schools and learning centres. Secondly, neo-conservatives who wish for a return to discipline and tradition in schools are influential in changes to the curriculum and educational outcomes. Thirdly, there is the influence of the professional and managerial middle class, which could also be seen as neo-liberalism; this group is committed to an audit culture, wants to measure efficiency, hold employees accountable and requires the constant production of evidence. While the final influence is clearly related to the demand for evidence of impact, each strand of influence is visible in education today and the first two influences affect who the education professionals are, how they are supported, the expectations placed on them and the culture in which they work.

As suggested above, value for money and accountability are not mutually exclusive when considering impact and the TDA's priorities for the professional development of the children's workforce in England (2009–2012) demonstrate this by bringing the two issues together in one of three priorities identified to improve quality and capacity: "All professional development [should be/ will be] judged and evaluated on its impact on children and young people and value for money..." (p.13). While the need for a link between professional development and pupils' learning and the need to ensure value for money has been identified (Ofsted, 2006), apart from in a minority of programmes, the impact of professional development has largely gone unchecked. Pedder et al., (2008) found that most school leaders, in considering impact, assess the extent to which activities address immediate school needs, collaborative working and the provision of new information as outcomes of professional development providing value for money. However, in a different systematic literature review Bolam and Weindling (2006) found that cost effectiveness and value for money are rarely taken into account when professional development provision is evaluated. Most evaluation of professional development activities by providers uses questionnaires and does not focus on clearly defined learning outcomes for teachers or pupils (Keay & Lloyd, 2008a) and while there is strong evidence in the literature that professional development can improve pupil learning, it is not often measured in terms of pupil achievement (Pedder et al., 2008). This issue is at the forefront of the proposals we make in this book for measuring the impact of professional development on children's learning and the problems relating to gathering evidence of impact are discussed in Chapter 6.

As mentioned above, in recent years increasing importance has been placed on teacher accountability with the introduction of professional standards tied to performance management. It could be assumed that having a clearer picture of the strengths and weaknesses of education professionals would lead to more focused professional development, but linking performance management and professional development is variable (Pedder et al., 2008) and the increasing expectation of accountability appears to have led to less individually focused professional development and more school-based, organisation focused development activities. There has been a strong drive for teachers to engage in school based professional development, which is linked to school development plans, with the expressed aim of improving the performance of the school. However, while children's and young people's learning is part of this picture, it is not at the centre of the identification of teachers' professional development needs. Burns (2005), found through education policy analysis that "... references to competencies and school development plans, knowledge and skills, show them to be part of the rhetoric of accountability, a top-down view of how change might be effected..." (p. 354). He explores the tensions created in a system where individual professional needs are subsumed and marginalised in the interests of improving the effectiveness and performance of institutions and the need to provide evidence that this improvement has taken place. These tensions are further compounded by the fact that much of the school based funding for professional development available to education professionals in England is externally controlled and tied to the introduction of new government initiatives, is often short term and takes the form of one off events, or short series of training events.

Control of Professional Development

Chapter 2 provides an examination of professionalism and its effects on professional development and control of individual action is identified as a major characteristic. Evetts (2009) writes about the discourse of professionalism, which can be analysed as a powerful instrument of occupational change and social control at macro (government), meso (school) and micro (individual) levels. Different versions of professionalism can be adopted, used and manipulated by individuals, schools and governments to both control and to avoid control. For example, Evetts (2003) suggests that there can be professionalism from within (manipulation of the market by the group) and from above (domination of forces external to the group). However, it is possible for both versions of professionalism to operate subversively and while outwardly appearing to give control or to be in control, in reality the reverse occurs. As illustrated in relation to professional development in the examples below:

- The school has total control of professional development
  No funding for professional development unless it is focused on school targets – individuals comply with this culture
- The individual has control of professional development
  Professional development is individually focused and funded by the school – the school sees professional development as an individual responsibility; there is no overall plan for professional development in place
- The school appears to have control of professional development but individuals subvert the system and its arrangements to ensure that they have access to the professional development they need/want. They appear to comply but in reality do not.
  Professional development activities are provided by the school and are either 'hi-jacked' to focus on staff needs or staff participate but little learning occurs e.g. some whole school INSET days.
- The individual appears to have control and responsibility but school resources are needed to participate and therefore the organisation really has control over the professional development.
  Professional development activities are not necessarily organised by the school but are funded and therefore only learning activities that contribute to school targets are supported.

None of these arrangements are wholly satisfactory or demonstrate an ideal model where development takes account of individual and organisational needs. In addition, there is also the macro influence of the Government, which must be taken into account. Alexandrou et al., (2005) present a set of complementary models for continuing professional development showing how it is possible to aim for the integration of systems led, profession led and individually led elements of professional development. This was developed as a result of research, which provided an overview of professional development in Europe and presents the issues in a very positive way, acknowledging that both individuals and systems, the Government and management of an organisation, have a vested interest in how education professionals are developed. However, they also suggest that the education profession should play a leading role in professional development and education professionals, as a group, should take control of their future and required development. This proposal raises questions about the locus of control and about whether professional development is primarily for the benefit of individual teachers, their schools or the Government: "Who is in control of the development is a crucial issue. Any approach to professional development which ignores this issue is missing a vital component" (Higgins and Leat, 1997, p.311) and a brief consideration, presented below, of how control of professional development has changed in England over the last 50 years emphasises this point.

Systems led professional development at an organisational level has developed over the last three decades and the role of schools/learning centres in defining their own professional development needs was promoted when an Inspectorate Survey Report (DES, 1977) signalled the fact that the teaching profession had grown beyond the stage of passive acceptance of INSET opportunities decided by others (Perry, 1980). However, school led professional development has grown at the expense of individually led development and staff development co-ordinators or head teachers have become the gatekeepers of professional development, making decisions about individual activity, based on funding and school priorities (Brown, Edmonds & Lee, 2001). In the same research, the School Development Plan played an important role in defining professional development activity and, unless it was written with input from all staff, it was only likely to reflect a narrow set of organisational priorities. Change to the allocation of funding, as a result of the devolution of budgets, has also been a catalyst for changing attitudes towards professional development provision. In a scenario where head teachers control the development budget, an individual teacher's development activity is unlikely to be funded unless it matches the needs of the school.

An historical overview of progressive government involvement in England demonstrates how prescription of practice and increased accountability have affected teachers' opportunities to engage in professional development. Reasons suggested for these changes centre on two projects, *raising standards* and *new public management*, which Bolam (1999) suggests are both treasury driven. *New public management* imports principles drawn from the private sector into the public sectors (Dunleavy & Hood, 1994) and Pring (2001) suggests that this situation is a reflection of changes in the management of all public services, not just education and not just in England. In the 1980s and 1990s, government policy brought about changes that reinforced a concern for accountability and, a change of government during this period made little difference to policy. However, Pring suggests that the intention in the action did change, from an interest in market driven initiatives, to one of accountability and responsibility, teachers' roles changed and government policy was continuing to control direction. For Beck (2008), the modernisation project of teachers has two main phases, initially from 1979 to 1997 teachers were discredited, some of them were portrayed as unprofessional while at the same time were increasingly held more accountable. Following this period, under New Labour, a new model of professionalism was constructed and winning teachers' support for it was the target. Using Bernstein's terms, he states that there was a weakening of the professional recontextualising field, research based knowledge, by using political powers to empower the official recontextualising field. Beck calls it governmental professionalism and claims that the TDA was employed to re-shape the official professional knowledge base.

The table below charts progressive changes in government control of professional development in England.

Table 3. Changes in government control of professional development for the education workforce in England

Phase	Changes to professional development for education professionals
1960 / 1970's	Professional development dominated by higher education provision and mainly concerned with funded secondments to higher degree award bearing courses.
1980's	Focus changed from individual development to school development. New funding methodologies influenced the changes and centrally retained funds were committed to government perceptions of teachers' training needs. TRIST (Technical and Vocational Education Initiative Related In-Service Training) brought focus on technical and vocational education, an intermediate step between the higher education (HE) dominated model and the school priority model of professional development provision)
1987	The Teachers' Pay and Conditions Act introduced five compulsory school-based training days.
1988	Shift in balance between government and professionals signalled in the Education Reform Act.
1990's	Professional development responsibilities for Local Education Authorities (LEA) and HE changed. LEAs' relationships with schools became less advisory and more focused on inspection and advisors became marginalised from the schools. Professional development provision in HE was limited by TTA funding policies (award bearing inset programme, 1998) that linked university based provision to national priorities. Introduction of an open bidding process. Change in funding direct to schools cutting out LEAs meant disbanding of the LEA advisory and inspection services and that in turn led to growth in number of independent providers. This was also influenced by the introduction of Ofsted inspections The school reform agenda. Demise in teacher renewal, with the emphasis on coping rather than developing. Teachers reported tensions existing between individual and school priorities and a diminishing sense of agency and control.
2000	National College for School Leadership introduced
2003	Remodelling of the education workforce. Planning, Preparation and Assessment (PPA) time (10% of timetabled teaching commitment to enable teachers to raise standards through individual or collaborative professional activity) Joint review by TDA and DfES recommended the need to monitor the impact of professional development courses.
2004 onwards	Postgraduate Professional Development funding, distributed to HEIs that applied and met criteria. TDA took on central responsibility for coordinating professional development for teachers (2006) Growth in the number of private companies providing professional development.
(Helsby, 1999; Law, 1999; Helsby, 1995; Pring, 2001; Brown et al., 2001; Day, 2000; Day, 2002; Forde et al., 2006)	

Changes from the 1980s onwards have meant that education professionals have concentrated on the practical issues of how to teach, i.e. the acquisition of *craft* knowledge, rather than the more theoretical questions about why and what to teach, i.e. *expert* and *pedagogical* knowledge (Helsby, 1995; Bolam, 1999). Although this was 10 years ago, our recent research (Keay & Lloyd, 2009) with professional development providers confirmed that when selecting professional development, a tips for teachers approach is still prioritised by providers and participants. Growing tensions between school-managed institutional development, group development and individual professional development (Law, 1999; Higgins & Leat, 1997) first identified in the 1990s, further illustrate changes in the control of professional development provision. This situation has not changed in the last decade and, with the current economic challenges, control of access to professional development opportunities and their focus does not seem likely to change in the foreseeable future. However, despite the fact that education professionals appear to have less control over their own work and development there is still an expectation that they act as professionals in the traditional way, exercising a degree of autonomy, demonstrating considerable commitment and providing evidence of their impact on children's learning (TDA, 2007).

Current Thinking On Impact

A critical review of literature and research on the impact of professional development demonstrates that while there is considerable concern amongst education professionals, researchers and writers about the impact of professional development, for the most part the emphasis is on the participants i.e. education professionals rather than the end users, the children, and their learning. Zeichner (2005) in presenting a research agenda for teacher education suggests that student learning has been largely neglected in teacher education research literature and goes on to suggest that we need broader conceptions of how to measure student competence or success as much of the research uses standardized tests. In a review of literature in New Zealand, Timperley et al., (2007) suggest that little is known about how teachers interpret learning, how they use new skills or the impact of them on teaching practice and student outcomes. Writers in the field acknowledge impact on practice as an important outcome of professional development and some do include pupil learning in a list of outcomes, for example,

> Professional development programs are systematic efforts to bring about change in the classroom practices of teachers, in their attitudes and beliefs, and in the learning outcomes of students. (Guskey, 2002, p. 381)

As far back as 1997 Harland and Kinder proposed a typology of nine INSET outcomes and suggested that 'impact on practice' is the ultimate goal, however, impact on practice does not necessarily mean impact on children's learning. Brown, Edmonds and Lee (2001) asked questions of teachers about the impact of professional development on their teaching and children's learning. Their findings are not surprising but serve to reinforce the difficult nature of assessing the impact of any professional development activity. They found that:

> There was an assumption that CPD would have an impact in school, on teachers, in the classroom and on children's learning.
>
> It was easier for teachers to identify impact on teaching than on learning.
>
> CPD led to increased confidence for teachers.
>
> Monitoring the impact of CPD is usually informal.
>
> Impact was felt at a school and individual level.
>
> Determining a direct link between CPD and impact was difficult as tangible evidence was not always readily available (Brown, Edmonds & Lee, 2001, p.87)

The issue of impact of professional development on practice has also been recognised as problematic internationally and a number of reports (Ingvarson et al., 2005; Bubb et al., 2008; Pedder et al., 2008; Darling-Hammond et al., 2009; Lawless & Pelegrino, 2007; Timperley et al., 2007) refer to the issue and the difficulties encountered by managers and teachers. There is no doubt that school reform and professional development are related and improvement in student learning is the ultimate aim of professional development (Bolam, 2000; Powell et al., 2002). However, Lawless & Pelegrino (2007) in a USA based focused review of research into the evaluation of professional development found that few studies used impact on pupil outcomes as a measurement of its effectiveness. Pedder et al., (2008) in their State of the Nation Report (2008) provide further evidence that the link between professional development and pupils' learning achievements in current research is weak and highlight the: "ambivalent nature of evidence in the literature related to links between CPD and pupils' learning achievements" (p.8). The problem may relate to the timing of the identification of intended impact; an inspection report from England stated that few schools evaluated the impact of professional development on teaching and learning effectively and suggested that one of the main reasons for this was that they failed to identify intended outcomes and suitable evaluation methods at the planning stage.

A review of recent research about issues relating to impact and evidence of impact (Burchell, Dyson & Rees, 2002; Lyle, 2003; Baumfield & Butterworth, 2005; Burns, 2005; Baumfield, 2006; Ingvarson et al., 2005; Goldschmidt & Phelps, 2010) reveals that while a number of projects have been set up to investigate it, they are, for the most part, concerned with the impact of professional development on teachers and their practice and learning and on school improvement and effectiveness rather than on pupils' learning. Other projects that recognise the link between professional development and student outcomes as important have focused on the types of professional development that have had an impact on student achievement. The model we have developed, and present in this book, approaches the issue of impact, not from the perspective of the learning activity but from the learning of the child.

While changes have been identified in learning processes in the classroom as a result of professional development, the issue of measuring the impact of these changes on the pupils' learning is not addressed beyond making general claims of the causal variety. Several research reports demonstrate this deficit, for example, McCormick et al., (2008) found strong evidence that professional development can improve pupils' learning but few studies were able to show evidence in terms of pupils' achievement and where they did attempt to do this the evidence was based on views of those involved and not on specific measures. Reporting on teachers' views about the effectiveness of award bearing professional development, MacDonald Grieve and McGinley (2010) found that teachers spoke about their professional development having made a wide ranging impact on their classroom practice and catering for pupils' needs, but did not provide evidence of impact. Cordingley (2008) found plenty of guidance about designing professional development around targeted student outcomes but little evidence of its impact or the production of hard data to quantify the effects of changing practice on students.

Research with professional development providers (Keay & Lloyd, 2008a) found that they did not consider children as stakeholders in teachers' professional development and in a national research project investigating teachers being prepared to cascade professional development to colleagues in their local authorities (Keay & Lloyd, 2008b) as suggested in Chapter 4, it became clear that the participants related impact to policy outcomes rather than to children's development. Many providers did not recognise the importance of end-users at all in their provision, but frequently focused on the needs of participants and the link is not made between the participants' and their pupils' learning. In both pieces of research while they acknowledged the importance of recognising the impact of development activities on children, the participants struggled with questions about what counts as evidence of impact and how it might be gathered. In summary, some research focuses on the impact of professional development on education professionals, other research focuses on its impact on pupils, but very little research focuses on the impact of professional development on pupils' learning and achievement. It is this relationship that the model presented in this book seeks to address.

Case study: Postgraduate Professional Development

In 2005, a model of long term professional development for qualified teachers was introduced by the TDA, through funding for Post-Graduate Professional Development (PPD) programmes, which was underpinned by a requirement for evidence of impact on performance and not just on the performance of the professionals and their schools but also on that of their pupils. Inevitably this has given rise to real concern amongst providers of professional development, schools and teachers about what counts as impact, how it can be measured and what counts as evidence of impact and in the first year of the programme there was resistance to including pupil outcomes in the PPD evaluation (Centre for the Use of Research and Evidence in Education (CUREE), 2010). Indeed, in previous research projects, referred to above, (Keay & Lloyd, 2008a; Keay & Lloyd, 2008b) the providers and education professionals considered these questions to be paramount amongst their concerns about measuring the impact of professional development provision.

The 2007 PPD Impact Evaluation Report (TDA) reinforces these concerns and makes clear that there are number of problematic issues for teachers and PPD providers with regard to the definition of what counts as evidence of impact on pupils' performance. The main criticism being that "a substantial minority of providers link teacher development and improved pupils' learning experience primarily through assertion i.e. that the first will automatically lead to the second" (p. 2). The report points to the nature of such causal links as a problem, which it says is also identified by many teachers and professional development providers themselves. The most recent report (TDA, 2009), based on the experiences of 25,000 teachers, confirms that while impact evaluation has taken 'centre stage' and that many providers now judge the ultimate success of their programmes in terms of the benefits for children and young people, the same problem remains. However, caution is still expressed by teachers participating in the programmes about making links between their professional development and subsequent pupil learning.

The evidence cited in the programme impact evaluation reports is often self reported by teachers and therefore limited to one source and programme providers also reported that it was easier to identify outcomes of the professional development in terms of pupils' experiences or impact on the participants and their approach to teaching rather than outcomes related to the pupils' academic achievement. However, the programme quality assurance overview (CUREE, 2010) reports that teachers are starting to consider impact on small groups instead of large classes, which suggests that they may be starting to think in terms of pupils' individual needs rather than always seeing them as a class. They also report that teachers are starting to make more use of children's voices to determine needs and have involved them in research.

While the PPD programme is making some progress on this issue, many thousands of teachers in the UK are choosing to engage with a variety of professional development, which is outside this programme, and may not be considering pupils' learning needs as an issue. Some professional development providers are aware of the need to consider the impact of their provision but for many it is not addressed adequately in their practice (Keay & Lloyd, 2008a). There is evidence to suggest that providers need help to develop more sophisticated methods to measure the impact of their provision as they tend to place emphasis on easily measurable outcomes or anecdotal evidence (ibid).

Why Should Education Professionals Measure the Impact of their Professional Development?

Despite the fact that this question should not need to be asked, the fact remains that many education professionals do not engage in professional development activities and if they do, may not seriously consider the impact of their learning on themselves or on the children in their classes. As discussed in Chapter 2, for many, professional development is seen to be a course and selection of development activities is often unrelated to a needs analysis and planning. Participation in development activities often happens by accident or due to convenience; a flyer on the staffroom coffee table, a chance discussion with another member of staff, a skills gap in the school or simply a whole school development event can all result in participation in unplanned, and possibly unnecessary professional development. In situations like this, where development activities are dislocated from individual professional needs, it is understandable, but not acceptable, that participants will not consider the impact of their professional development beyond their own learning.

Although engagement in professional development and an obligation to keep up to date with skills and knowledge are linked with professional progression, engagement in professional development is varied and often relies on an individual's ability to access activities and the necessary funding. The recent Select Committee Report on Education in England found that there is not a strong enough culture of professional development within the education workforce and attributes this to poor access to opportunities and lack of funding. However, some teachers do undertake professional development on a regular basis and see it having an impact on their roles and particular areas identified by Pedder et al., (2008) are professional skills and knowledge (77%) and increased awareness of teaching and learning issues (71%). 63% of teachers in their survey believed that professional development activities improve pupil performance, 59% reported impact on pupils' learning practices as a result of professional development and some also reported improvements in behaviour or classroom climate. So evaluating the impact of professional development on practice can be motivating and as Cordingley et al., (2005) suggest, pupil impact can motivate teachers to sustain their learning and will encourage further development.

In addition to regulatory requirements to meet professional standards or performance targets, evaluating the impact of new professional learning is essential to ensure that the value of the investment is clear. This refers not only to the financial resource invested by the individual's organisation but also to the time invested in participating in the learning activity and putting new learning into practice. In order to be clear that the investment has been worthwhile, the selection of development activity must be purposeful, part of the process of development planning and relevant to the individual's occupational context.

So, while measuring the impact of professional development is professionally motivating and provides an evaluation of investment, the most important answer to the question asked at the beginning of this section, involves the children, the end-users of professional development. It is a matter of self-respect and as Malm (2009) suggests, anyone working in schools or learning centres owes it to the children to be the best she/he can. The McKinsey Report (Barber & Mourshed, 2007) on the best performing school systems states that teachers are important and are the main drivers of variation in student learning, therefore, good teaching should lead to the inclusive educational outcomes for students, as identified in Chapter 3. Pupils constantly set challenges for those who work with them and the education workforce must meet those challenges.

Impact Driven Professional Development

Naturally, there are dangers in imposing an impact driven model of professional development and as we have engaged in developing the process model, presented in this book, we have been very aware of the possibility of a reductionist model emerging. Impact seen purely in terms of easily measurable outcomes such as standardised scores and tests is not what we propose. However, some of these measurable outcomes may be very useful if they demonstrate specific learning in the classroom.

Other challenges that must be acknowledged include the range of development opportunities that may, or may not be, available and as Hodkinson (2009) found, money was available for activities that were targeted at government imposed priorities and the school's development plan and this appears to be the case in many schools. Teachers who have accessed funding for PPD have told us that without the resource provided through this scheme, they would not be able to afford to participate. Variable funding across educational establishments, access to high quality professional development experiences, time to participate and cover for classes if the activity is during working hours are all barriers to professional development and consequently pupils' learning. However, as Timperley et al., (2007) found, conditions that promote learning are complex:

> Extended opportunities to learn, however, are not necessarily more effective than their one-off counterparts. Two extremes that are sometimes portrayed as effective have little evidence to support them. The first is that teachers should be treated as self-regulating professionals who, if given sufficient time and resources, are able to construct their own learning experiences and develop a more effective reality for their students through their collective expertise. Unfortunately, we found little evidence to support the claim that providing teachers with time and resources is effective in promoting professional learning in ways that have positive outcomes for students. (p.xxv)

If we are aware of the barriers, and the complexity of learning conditions, impact driven professional development may contribute to improving the education workforce. It can counter under performance by integrating performance management and individual development planning. It can ensure value for money, a focus on learning for adult and child and improved learning outcomes that we are clear have been achieved. It can also ensure support for professional development and, as explored in more detail in Chapter 7, it can help individuals to access a range of appropriate professional development. Ultimately, it has the potential to achieve a better education workforce. We must stress at this point that all the suggestions we make for using the process model are driven by the desire to improve children's learning and not to introduce another mechanism to address performance issues. While we cannot not deny the importance of ensuring that teachers are effective, we believe that a democratic approach to professionalism where classroom professionals take responsibility for their own learning and subsequent impact on children's learning will be more effective.

Effective Professional Development

If professional development is to have an impact on children's learning it must be effective and this section of the chapter develops the essential ingredients that can be seen to be indicators of high quality professional development that were presented in Chapter 4. These indicators of effectiveness have informed the development of the process model presented in Chapter 7. The following points have been developed through our own research and with reference to several large scale international research reviews which examined professional development and its effectiveness (Cordingley et al., 2003; Timperley et al., Pedder et al., 2008; Darling-Hammond et al., 2009; Doecke et al., 2008, Scheerens et al., 2010).

Professional development is most effective when:

- The *culture* of the organisation expects development, supports it and promotes it within a learning community.
- Education professionals *control* and take *responsibility* for identifying and meeting their own professional development needs.
- Learning targets go beyond *relevance* to organisational context to ensure that individuals take into account their own needs in relation to the needs of their pupils.
- Learning activities are *personalised* and *progressive,* focusing on individual needs and building on existing expertise.
- Professional development activities reflect a *range of opportunities*, which recognise where expertise and support may best be found.

One of the most important elements is the relevance of professional development to pupils and Guskey (2002) proposes that changes to teachers' beliefs and attitudes, towards the effectiveness of the professional development they have engaged in, are only achieved when they have evidence that the change in their classroom practice has resulted in student learning. Professional development episodes often attempt to firstly change attitudes towards the professional development and win teachers over, then to get them to change practice to see improved outcomes. The model presented in Chapter 7 reverses that process; the impact of professional development is not in evidence until beliefs and attitudes are changed as a result of seeing improved student learning.

CHAPTER SUMMARY

This chapter has discussed the interest in impact and identified two major forces in considering the impact of professional development, value for money and accountability. The need for classroom professionals to control their own development has been promoted but is contextualised within a history of political interest and regulatory demands. While writers in this area have promoted the importance of linking professional development and pupils' learning and the benefits of engaging in a process that does this are clear, previous research demonstrates a lack of focus on the issue of providing evidence of impact. Putting the needs of children at the centre of teachers' professional development through a process of identification and impact analysis has the potential to give genuine substance to critically reflective practice, an expectation placed on teachers but one which is not always met. There are, therefore, two questions which now require exploration.

− What sort of evidence do classroom professionals need to collect to demonstrate that professional development had been effective?
− What process will enable teachers to identify their own professional development needs in relation to the learning needs of pupils?

LEARNING AND TEACHING - GATHERING EVIDENCE OF IMPACT ON LEARNING

The identification of impact, and what counts as evidence of impact, on pupils' learning, is inextricably linked to effective monitoring, assessment and evaluation of learning. This chapter will further develop the discussion in Chapter 3 about inclusive approaches to learning, teaching and assessment, which enable and support the impact driven model of professional development presented in this book and discussed in detail in Chapter 7. It will also address the need for education professionals working towards more inclusive approaches to teaching and learning to expand their understanding of what is meant by success and achievement. The identification of the learning needs of learners and their teachers is crucial to the model and therefore approaches to learning and teaching, which support and enable effective identification processes, will also be discussed. Evidence required to demonstrate that the identified learning needs have been met, the form it will take and how it will be collected are also key features of the model and this chapter will present a critical discussion about what counts as evidence of impact and about different types of evidence.

THE LEARNER AND LEARNING

The model of impact driven professional development proposed in this book requires that education professionals are able to identify and understand the learning needs of pupils and to make appropriate and relevant choices about their learning and professional development needs, necessary to enable them to address their pupils' learning needs effectively. In order to measure the impact of their professional development on the pupils' learning they also need to be able to decide what will count as evidence that learning has taken place and to implement effective assessment and evaluation processes to collect that evidence. As discussed in relation to the development of more inclusive practice in Chapter 3, this requires that they adopt a view which places the learner at the centre of the education process. It also requires the adoption an approach to learning, for the pupil and for themselves, which is active, flexible, self initiated and empowering and which commences with the assessment and identification of what learners *can* do rather than what they *cannot* do. This model of learning and the learner, based on the idea that education should be child or learner centred, is inspired by the work of such educationalists as Dewey, (1963), Bruner (1986), Stenhouse (1986), Rogers (1967) and Friere (1973). It is an approach founded on learning as an active engagement with a carefully managed, challenging learning environment where the role of the teacher, other education professionals and agencies is to support, facilitate and enable the process collaboratively. The voice and intentions of the learner are also important in determining learning needs and intended learning targets and outcomes, which are inevitably tentative, open and individual. One of the aims of the education process is that learners will be motivated to take responsibility for their own learning in a negotiated consultation with their teachers and a range of other relevant partners including parents and support professionals. Morgan (2009) emphasises the importance of this sort of consultation process to the development of genuinely informed learning and teaching.

> Consultation offers a way for teachers and pupils to engage with each other in dialogue and develop dynamic partnerships which pave the way for effective teaching and learning. The challenge for schools and policy-makers is to create the conditions which will enable this to take place and to support teachers to implement effective and enabling strategies of consultation on teaching and learning with their pupils. (p.20)

This approach not only presents challenges for schools and policy makers, it also challenges education professionals, to see themselves as learners, collaborating and negotiating, with the pupils and with each other in the project of learning. In the words of Williamson and Morgan (2009),

> This means, for teachers, finding ways to listen and appreciate the varieties of children's experiences, and then to identify intelligent and practical classroom responses which enable children to make sense of those experiences and the factors that influence them. (p. 293)

While the adoption of this approach may, indeed, present a range of challenges it is clear that this sort of negotiated, problem sharing, collaborative and empowering approach to learning has the potential to support and enable much more effective identification of pupils' *genuine* individual learning needs. It puts the learning and the learning needs of the child at the centre of the process rather than the need to perform well in standardized tests or to fulfil the curricular requirements. It is also an approach, which inevitably facilitates far deeper understanding of the pupils' learning processes and how they might be supported and enabled. In addition, this partnership approach to identifying what and how pupils learn and can be supported to learn is inevitably motivating for everyone involved. It can also be seen as a prerequisite for inclusion and the development of inclusive practice and may go a long way towards addressing many of the problems and issues raised and discussed in Chapter 3.

> Celebrating difference as enrichment and the development of approaches to the curriculum which value what children *can* do rather than emphasising what they *can't* do; empowering pupils to take responsibility for their own learning and enabling them to participate more fully in society; and the development of collaborative networks of teacher who are able to engage jointly in problem-solving can all be seen as prerequisites for the development of genuinely inclusive practice. (Lloyd, 2002, p.124)

It is interesting to note that recent policy in education in England has also been promoting a model of learning and the learner which would seem to be very much along the lines of that described above. *2020 vision*, also known as the Gilbert Review (2006), describes an appropriate and relevant model of the learner and learning for high quality education in the 21st Century, in the following way:

> Close attention is paid to learners' knowledge, skills, understanding and attitudes. Learning is connected to what they already know (including from outside the classroom). Teaching enthuses pupils and engages their interest in learning: it identifies, explores and corrects misconceptions. Learners are active and curious: they create their own hypotheses, ask their own questions, coach one another, set goals for themselves, monitor their progress and experiment with ideas for taking risks. (p.6)

The Review goes on to recommend that the route through which to ensure this approach to the learner and learning is through personalising learning and teaching so that every child receives an education that meets his/her needs. At face value the Review seems, then, to be calling for the sort of learner/child centred approach suggested above. However Williamson and Morgan (2009) point to considerable criticism of the personalisation agenda and its growing rhetoric in policy and practice in education not only in England but further afield.

The Personalisation Agenda

Hartley (2009) identifies a very clear difference between learner/child centred, individualised approaches to education and pedagogy, which are rooted in a theory of learning and supported by credible academic research and the personalisation agenda, as recently promoted in education policy, which he says finds its roots in marketing theory. He points out that Government has made very clear that it is not suggesting the adoption of a child centred approach, often associated with the, so called, progressive approaches employed in the 60s and 70s, with its personalisation agenda. Nevertheless, according to Hartley, there seems to be a deliberate blurring of terminology. Which he proposes is used to give the personalisation agenda more credibility and raise it to the status of a pedagogical approach, which he maintains it most certainly is not:

> By retaining the term personalisation the government purports to do two things: first because of its focus on personalised 'tailored' needs and co-produced solutions, it adapts education even further to a consumerist society; and second, because the term personalisation strikes a chord with the discourse of child-centred education, it blurs the fact that little to do with pedagogy of the curriculum has in fact been changed. (p. 423)

Indeed close examination of the term as promoted in *2020 vision* (2006), makes clear that personalising teaching and learning are not about being learner or child centred, as described above, but more about promoting school effectiveness, improving performance in terms of existing standards and indeed maintaining the status quo in relation to the National Curriculum and its associated testing procedures. While there is a great deal of emphasis placed on tailoring learning to meet the needs of the individual, these needs are to be identified, not in relation to the individual, but in relation to his/her performance with the existing standardised tests and curricula, seen as the vehicle through which education and learning for all can be best achieved. Extending the tailoring metaphor Hartley (2008) makes the point that,

> Notwithstanding the talk of tailoring education to the needs of the individual, what we have so far is not bespoke tailoring, but rather alterations to an off-the-peg garment...Perhaps all this is no more than an intentionally cautious first move by government, a transition stage; or perhaps government wishes simply to use the consumerist slogan of personalization as a legitimacy rhetoric to mask its continuing 'system-designer' role, thereby containing (through its 'national' this and that) the centrifugal forces of contemporary consumer culture. As matters stand, we have a 'weak' version of personalisation, which in marketing terms amounts to little more than a makeover. (p. 379)

For teachers and education professionals a new set of standards relating to the skills for personalised learning is proposed in *2020 vision* (2006), which is also linked to performance in terms of the standards and performance management procedures. Williamson and Morgan (2009) point out, however, that,

> The current logic of personalisation as a pedagogy that can be schematised and diagrammatised according to phases of institutional completion neglects...treats personalisation as a classroom craft that can be achieved by the simple manufacturing of a few pedagogical techniques....Changing professional practices requires the breaking down of powerful habits of thinking and behaving. When schools take innovations, they do so in ways that reflect their own values and missions. The sustainability of such changes depends on teachers possessing an understanding of the moral and political factors that are influencing their personal practices. (p. 301)

It is therefore important that education professionals are able to understand and are fully aware of the implications of personalisation policy, and are able to critique it rigorously, in order that they can recognise its scope and limitations for their practice before deciding whether it is appropriate to make changes. It is also vitally important, for the success of the model of impact driven professional development presented in this book, that they are able to distinguish between the notion of learner/child centred approaches to learning and teaching which support and enable them to identify, address and evaluate the *genuine* individual learning needs of their pupils, and personalised learning, as criticised above, which focuses on the curriculum, standardised tests and assessment and performance of pupils and teachers as the means to identify learning needs. These problematic and important issues, as well as others, relating to the professional development needs arising as a result of this policy are also discussed in Chapter 2 in relation to the professional learning. It is important to note that in spite of the criticisms discussed above, and also taking account that at the time of writing we have a relatively new government in England, a Conservative/Liberal alliance, which, although it seems unlikely, might result in changes to approaches being adopted in education policy relating to learning and teaching, there is no doubt that the notion of personalisation has taken a powerful hold and has become a driving force in education policy relating to learning teaching and assessment, not just in England but also further afield (Crick, 2009).

Identifying Learning Needs

Some of the criticisms above relating to the personalisation agenda, as promoted in recent and current education policy, can also, to an extent, be related to the notion of individualised learning and planning. This can certainly be seen to be the case where the Individual Education Plan (IEP), is used, for example, as a device to legitimise a 'watered down' version of learning or to separate out pupils whose learning or behaviour do not meet the level or standard stipulated by the National Curriculum and/or testing procedures for their age and stage (Benjamin, 2002; Lloyd, 2008). In this case the use of the IEP can be seen to have little to do with the learner/child centred approach discussed at the beginning of this chapter and is open to the same criticisms as those presented above in relation to 'tailored' learning. It is important to note that the notion of individualised learning used as complementary, or even interchangeably, with personalisation is not compatible with the learner/child centred, inclusive approach we believe to be necessary for the success of the impact driven model of professional development promoted by this book.

It should be recognised that the effective identification of pupils' *genuine* learning needs is not an easy task. Clearly there are a number of competing factors which can be seen to militate against it including pressures of standardised norm/age related tests; the demands of delivering the National Curriculum; the wider range of ability in mainstream classrooms as a result of recent policy for inclusion; and feelings of inadequacy in terms of knowledge and expertise amongst education professionals. As a result, pupils' learning needs are often identified in relation to the generic norms of the key stages of the curriculum at which they are operating or to the standardised tests they will be expected to pass or to some kind of received wisdom about what is *normal* for a child to achieve at a given age or stage in maturation. Much discussion is also taking place, currently, about the skills and knowledge necessary for the economic success of the UK and society in the 21st Century, as for example in the Leitch Report (2006). This has also led to pupils'/students' learning needs being defined not in terms of their own learning but in terms of the needs of society and their usefulness to society and the economy and can be seen as a particularly powerful influence on education (Ball 2008; Barber, 2008).

For the model of impact driven professional development presented in this book the effective identification of pupils' *genuine* learning needs is the starting point for ensuring that learning does actually take place and for making decisions about what interventions are necessary in order to ensure that it does. It is also the starting point from which progress, success and achievement can be assessed and measured and evidence of impact collected. The model requires a sensitive process through which the teacher and other education professionals involved are able to identify the learning which has already taken place, and using what has already been achieved, employ the sort of collaborative negotiation discussed earlier, with the pupil and other relevant agencies, to identify further learning needs and to set targets for that learning to take place. This sort of process is not easy to achieve and not only do education professionals need to develop their skills and abilities to make it effective but also the pupils themselves need support and opportunities to enable them to articulate what they already know, to negotiate what they need to learn and to reach consensus about targets for learning. These are sophisticated skills and abilities and can only be learnt through engaging with them. Lloyd and Beard (1995), discussing a longitudinal project, informed by the learner/child centred approach discussed above, which set out to develop active, self directed, empowering learning, point to the importance of being able to observe and assess pupils engaging with each other in a range of activities in order to understand what they really are able to do and to collect meaningful and invaluable information and evidence to support these assertions. The learning and teaching strategy employed during the project included a carefully balanced and managed mix of whole class, individual and small group learning opportunities geared towards the development of interactive, collaborative learning. It centred on the development of the individual skills and abilities necessary for pupils to engage with each other, their teachers and with problem sharing, investigative learning. This approach

> …provides the opportunity for teachers to observe pupils and to assess and evaluate their understanding. It also releases teachers to watch and listen to their pupils interacting with each other and the task. The information which can be amassed about the pupils is both meaningful and invaluable in the process of designing further programmes of study to develop and extend them… it offers the opportunity to observe the process of pupils' thinking. Working in this way encourages children to verbalise the processes they are using to solve problems. They are engaged in explaining, hypothesising, discussing, arguing, reaching consensus, compromising, listening and a host of other activities, as well as producing solutions to the task. (p.13)

The authors make clear that managing the sort of interactive group work, which enables this sort of observation and data collection, requires rigor, structure and careful planning and organisation if it is to be effective and successful. Pupils need to be provided with an enabling structure and need to be taught and to learn the skills and the language necessary for effective collaboration. They need to be *emphasis*

engaged in a gradual process of taking responsibility for their own learning and to acquire the skills necessary to articulate what they have been doing and to share and critically reflect upon their experiences. They need to be involved in discussions about what they have learnt and in negotiations about what they need to learn and these discussions should centre on the processes of learning how to learn as well as content in terms of subject knowledge. This structure, organisation and the acquisition of skills also applies to the teacher(s) involved and much emphasis is placed on the value of collaborative teaching as well as collaborative learning. What is clear is that this sort of approach, which is rooted in the learning process and context, is learner focused and sees the teacher as a learner and partner in the teaching and learning process, has the potential to provide exactly the sort of information about the pupils' learning and learning processes necessary to make informed decisions about what they know and to negotiate with them what they need to learn. It also provides real opportunities for the identification of pupils' *genuine* learning needs. Inevitably this sort of approach to identifying learning needs has the potential to ensure that further planned learning is relevant, engaging and is more likely to lead to self initiated and directed learning. It also has the potential to assist teachers and other learning professionals with the difficult task of ensuring that *genuine* learning is taking place and to provide the means to assess and monitor that process more effectively.

Assessing Success and Achievement – Monitoring and Evaluating Learning

Effective assessment of pupils' learning is, of course, key to demonstrating that an impact has been made and that learning has indeed taken place. However, this raises issues about what counts as success and achievement in terms of learning and how success and achievement are measured. We have in place in the English education system, and indeed in most countries, systems of assessment and testing, which are norm, age, and standard related, and in England linked to pupils' performance in tests related to the levels and stages of the National Curriculum. Thus success and achievement are measured, for the most part, in terms of a set of predetermined standards which dictate what a pupil should know and be able to do at a particular age and stage of development and not in relation to his or her learning needs or processes. Assessment of learning, success and achievement is often seen as synonymous with a summative process of testing, at the end of a key stage or unit of work, which is used to provide information required for national reporting on the performance of schools and pupils. This approach alone inevitably leads to a narrowing of the concepts of success achievement. Clearly the assessment procedures of the national testing system in England, in relation to the National Curriculum are important and cannot be ignored but they are and must be seen as, only part of the picture. They cannot on their own provide the rich qualitative data teachers and education professionals require if they are to assess, effectively, the impact their teaching has had on pupils' learning. Nor do they provide data that can be used as evidence of that impact. *2020 vision* (2006) calls for an approach to assessment which recognises, not only this sort of summative assessment *of* pupils' learning, but also takes account of the motivational potential of assessment *for* learning:

> It is not an occasional activity at the end of a unit of work, but a complex, joint activity between the teacher and pupil. It helps teachers identify what pupils have or have not achieved, while pupils increase their understanding of the standard expected, their progress towards it and what they need to do to reach it. All this provides information to help the teachers to adjust their teaching. (p.16)

While the criticisms levelled at this Review earlier in this chapter can clearly be identified, once again, in this statement, in that the whole approach described can be seen to be more to do with the need to maintain the status quo with regard to national standards and criteria, the emphasis on assessment *for* learning, involving pupils, their teachers, parents and other education professionals is nevertheless welcome. It places importance on learning as a process and acknowledges the value of involving pupils themselves in assessing their own progress and also makes the point that this approach provides important information for teachers about what they need to know and learn themselves in order to ensure that their teaching is making an impact and enabling their pupils to progress in their learning. The involvement of pupils in the process of assessing their own learning progress is not only motivating, it also has the potential to inform their understanding about the learning process, in other words it provides opportunities for learning how to learn in addition to focusing on what they have learnt. It is, however, essential that the involvement of pupils in the assessment of their learning is supported and strategically managed if it is to be used effectively. Rose and Howley (2007) stress the importance of employing critical questioning and reflection strategies when asking pupils to assess what and how they have learnt. These are strategies which the teacher and the pupil must learn to employ for genuinely effective assessments to be carried out. Lloyd and Beard (1995) place emphasis on the need to provide the tools for involving pupils in their own assessment by teaching them the language and skills they need to understand and use in the process of evaluating what and how they have learnt, and the tasks they have engaged with in order to learn. This approach to assessment can also be seen to have the potential to expand understanding about what is meant by success and achievement. Emphasis on the processes of learning in addition to the content allows for the possibility that important learning is likely to take place even though the intended outcome of the teaching may not have been achieved. This affirming approach to learning, success and achievement is essential for the development of more inclusive education, as discussed in Chapter 3, as it adopts a process approach, allowing greater participation for a wider range of ability. Concentration on assessing and understanding the processes of learning with a view to improvement for the pupil and teacher and other education professionals, rather than on the outcomes in terms of performance by the pupil, measured or tested at the end of a stage or in unit tests, is inevitably more informative. It also places emphasis on the role of the teachers and other education professionals in the learning process and enables them to identify their contribution to it and to focus on gaps in their own understanding and learning. Providing opportunities for, and facilitating pupils' participation in, the processes of monitoring, assessing and evaluating their own learning can be seen, then, to be an excellent strategy for identifying evidence of the impact teaching is making.

What Counts as Impact on Learning for Pupils and Professionals?

Increased accountability tied to pupil performance over recent years in England has led to real concerns amongst education professionals about what counts as impact on pupils' learning and how to demonstrate evidence of that impact as discussed in relation to professional development in more detail, in Chapter 4. The TDA has recently raised concerns that there is still considerable confusion about what counts as evidence of impact on pupils' learning and points to the reliance on self reported evidence of impact which relates more to changes in teachers' performance and learning rather than pupils' learning outcomes (2009). The notion of impact implies a direct connection between an intervention and its outcome. In terms of teaching and learning, which are complex processes influenced and impacted upon by a wide range of factors, it is inevitably difficult and problematic to determine what counts as impact and indeed as evidence of that impact. Simplistic answers in terms of test scores and other such performance indicators fail to address the complexity of the interactions between the teacher and learner; learner and other learners; the learner and the learning content; the learner and the learning context and a whole range of other potentially influencing factors. Similarly, decisions about what counts as evidence of impact on learning are neither simple nor straightforward.

What is clear, from the discussion in the earlier sections of this chapter, is that a model of the learner and learning which adopts an approach to identifying pupils' *genuine* learning needs through a collaborative negotiated process involving the pupil, teacher and a range of other appropriate professionals and agencies, also provides an excellent starting point for determining what the intended impact of the learning should be. In addition, providing structured, carefully managed opportunities, of the sort suggested by Lloyd and Beard, (1995), for individual, small group and whole group learning, allows for the collection of rich qualitative information about the learner and learning processes and indeed the teacher and teaching processes. This data together with the information collected through the use of assessment and monitoring which are formative, flexible, rely on pupil participation and which centre around learning how to learn as well as the learning content, will, with careful interpretation, analysis and critical reflection, supply a wealth of useful and important evidence about those processes. Evidence collected in this way has enormous potential, not only for providing feedback with which to inform future learning and teaching for the pupils, but also for the learning of the teachers and other education professionals who engage in the process. In terms of demonstrating impact, the assessment process discussed earlier, where the rich information and evidence collected are interrogated and critically evaluated collaboratively together with the learner, has the potential to assist with this complex and problematic requirement. To exploit this potential, the focus for the identification of impact should be on providing evidence of a wide range of processes in relation, of course, to the initial learning needs identified. This might include, for example:

–   What has taken place in the learning and teaching processes?
–   What has been the role of the learner in this?
–   What interventions have been made by the teacher or others involved?
–   What content has been learnt?
–   What skills have been developed or learnt?

Collecting evidence of impact should not be for external accountability purposes alone but should be seen as an integral part of the evaluation process used to provide important information and feedback for further learning and teaching. Therefore it is important that evidence of impact should be identified in a wide and flexible variety of forms, such as, for example, reflective journals entries by pupils and teachers, examples of pupils' work, video clips, or recordings. Clearly this links back to the initial identification of learning needs. As the decisions about the learning and teaching which needs to take place and how that learning and teaching will take place are discussed and negotiated, what evidence will be produced to demonstrate impact on learning and what form it will take should also be decided as part of that process. Indeed the form the evidence takes and how it will be collected should be determined by the learning and teaching and how the learning and teaching will be implemented.

Implications for the Model

The four stage process of identifying, gathering and evaluating evidence through a collaborative negotiation between education professionals and their pupils/students, described and illustrated above, is integral and essential to the process model presented in this book. It is a process, which is underpinned by, and indeed is essential to, the development of the inclusive approach to practice discussed in Chapter 3. It supports the effective identification of pupils'/students' learning needs, discussed earlier in this chapter, which is essential for the successful use of the model because unless education professionals are able to identify and assess the learning needs of their pupils/students effectively they will be unable to identify their own learning needs in relation to them. The model is concerned with impact and with demonstrating impact through evidence. It is important to be very clear, however, that impact here refers to changed, developed and/or transformed learning and teaching, for the pupils/students and for the education professionals and is not measured in relation to organisational or externally imposed targets. Similarly the evidence required to demonstrate impact is qualitative and learning and learner centred and determined, as discussed above.

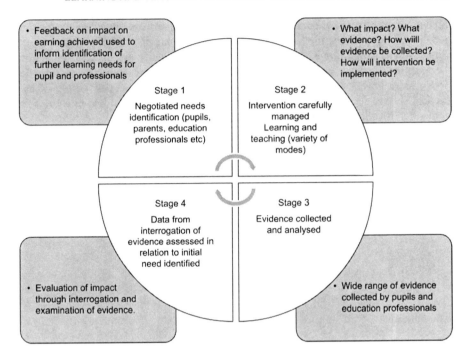

Figure 1. Collecting evidence of impact.

CHAPTER SUMMARY

This chapter has looked at an approach to the learner and learning which can facilitate and support the identification of pupils' *genuine* learning needs and which at the same time has the potential to provide teachers and other education professionals with evidence of impact on learning. This approach has been discussed in relation to the recent and current rhetoric of personalisation which can be identified as an increasingly popular policy agenda in education, in England and further afield. Personalisation as promoted in recent and current policy, however, seems to be more concerned with further establishing a market model of education with pupils and their parents as consumers of a pre determined, one size fits all, product than providing flexible educational opportunities which address the individual learning needs of the pupil. Indeed learning and teaching strategies, informed by a learner/child centred approach, which place the learner at the centre of the learning process, engaged and involved as an active participant in his/her own learning, can be seen to be essential if this is to be achieved. Such an approach requires that learning needs are identified, assessed, monitored and evaluated in a collaborative negotiation process with the learner, teacher and other appropriate professionals and agencies. This provides important opportunities to collect rich qualitative information about the learning and teaching process as well as the learner and the teacher and how they engage with the learning process. Through a process of critical interrogation this information can be used to identify evidence of impact on the learning process, which can be used to inform further learning, but also to demonstrate how and what learning has taken place. The processes described are cyclical so that decisions about what evidence should be collected and how are part of the identification, assessment and monitoring processes.

THE MODEL

Chapters 1–6 explore concepts relating to teaching and learning and what we believe to be the essential ingredients for high quality and effective professional development. The purpose of this exploration is to provide a theoretical background and justification for the process model presented in detail in this chapter. The model is underpinned by an inclusive approach to educational practice for all children, employed by professionals who work within educational cultures, which actively promote, and expect, transformative professionalism. Professional development undertaken within the model must be planned and consist of a broad range of activities through which all education professionals involved in the development processes consider the impact of their contribution and the evidence required to demonstrate its effectiveness. It is important at this stage to reiterate that we are not advocating that education professionals should only undertake professional development identified through this process. We acknowledge that there will be other justifications for professional development, which will be linked to career developments, for example, management programmes, higher degrees or the demands of a new role. This chapter presents an overview of the research process undertaken to develop the model and the stages of its development, a critical examination of the context and culture required in schools/centres to ensure that the model will be effective, and concludes with an analysis of the questions education professionals must ask themselves if this model is to become embedded within their professional practice and learning.

DEVELOPING THE PROCESS MODEL

Research Approach

A grounded theory approach was adopted to develop the process model over a period of three years and an analysis framework, based on Strauss and Corbin's (1998) work, which divided the process into three stages, *ideas, action and resulting theory*, was employed. The *ideas* stage involved further analysis of data generated in previous research, through which it had become clear that there was a problem around impact and evidence. The previous research consisted of three projects, each of which took place over several years. These projects investigated the promotion of high quality professional development with a range of providers; undertook an evaluation of a model of professional development, which expected participants to cascade information in their own organisations; and explored the professional development experiences of new teachers. In addition to these projects we also undertook two other short-term projects focusing on professional development, which informed the ideas stage of the research. While all of these projects were clearly influential in the development of the model, we have engaged in research and enquiry in the field of education for more than twenty years and the development of the model can be seen as organic as we have drawn on the results of previous professional experiences, research and projects to inform its development. The details of each major project that we consider to have informed the initial model development are presented in an appendix to this book.

The previous research provided a starting point for a process which is, as mentioned above, a form of grounded theory. While it was primarily inductive, a process described by users of this approach, in that it aimed to develop theory, it took the form of an interplay of induction and deduction; Keay (2006) provides a more detailed explanation of this approach to grounded theory. This approach acknowledges that we cannot come to research devoid of ideas and that previous research has informed the *ideas*. Thomas and James (2006) raise this issue in their critique of grounded theory and refer to the views of biologist Peter Medawar, who suggests that using both induction and deduction has the potential to ensure a more rigorous process. In the development of the process model the *action* and *resulting theory* stages were symbolic of this interplay as each stage of the research involved returning to the model to revise ideas that were then used in subsequent developments of the model and in the research activities used to pilot each development. This approach recognises that both interpretive and positivist traditions can be used in undertaking a grounded theory approach.

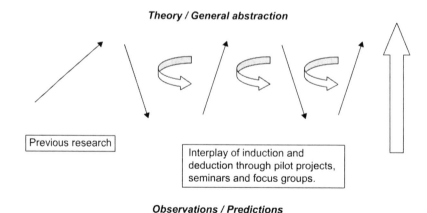

Figure 2. Continuous interplay between induction and deduction during the development of the process model.

There are inevitably drawbacks to adopting a grounded theory approach (e.g. Layder, 1993, Hammersley, 1992) and Thomas and James (2006, p. 768), summarise them in three broad themes, i) grounded theory oversimplifies complex meanings and inter-relationships in the data; ii) it constrains analysis, putting procedure before interpretation; and iii) it depends upon inappropriate models of induction and asserts from them inappropriate claims to explanation and prediction. The notion of induction is not universally accepted, for example, Gorard (2001) cites the problem of its 'shaky philosophical foundation' and refers to theorists such as Popper who question the existence of inductive logic. Related to this, there is confusion concerning the character of grounded theorising and it has been criticised as 'inductivist positivism'. Hammersley (1992) suggests that there is some ambiguity in the writings of Glaser and Strauss concerning the relationship between 'grounded theorising' and a 'hypothetico-deductive' mode of research. He states that 'grounded theorising' and 'analytical induction' are attempts to apply a 'hypothetico-deductive' method to ethnography, and that neither is very effective. However, Glaser and Strauss (1967) make it very clear that 'grounded theorising' is very much concerned with generating theory from data and freeing the researcher from merely verifying 'grand theory'.

The process of developing the model did, after the initial stages, involve the use of research to develop theory and explore the hypotheses generated from prior data collection. Strauss and Corbin (1998) acknowledge the interplay between induction and deduction and believe that interpreting data is a form of deduction. They also highlight that data is not interpreted in a clinical manner and this was evident in the way our own assumptions, the literature that we have read and discussions we had with colleagues all influenced the outcomes. As Hammersley suggests, "…all research involves both deduction and induction in the broad senses of those terms; in all research we move from ideas to data as well as from data to ideas" (1992, p.168).

Data Collection

As described above and shown in Figure 2 a range of data collection methods and discussion forums were used to pilot successive versions of the model and to test the underpinning theories. Presentation of the ideas and the model at international conferences over three years, invitations to present to masters and doctoral students on the topic and specifically formed focus groups, including teachers, managers and professional development providers, to discuss the model, all informed its development. In the later stages of development we undertook three pilot studies in education institutions, which provided the opportunities to gather the views of a range of education professionals in early years, primary, secondary and special education settings. In the final stages of developing the model we returned to the context, which had originally provided the impetus for this journey, the PDB-PE and a document analysis of recent applications for recognition, by professional development providers, to the Board was undertaken and the final version of the model was piloted with a group of providers.

Pilot studies took place in three school/learning centres with groups of education professionals who volunteered to work through and provide feedback about the process model, its usefulness and their professional development experiences while using it. The approach used can be described as practice-based participative enquiry because the participants were fully involved in the research and it was based firmly in their every day practice.

Pilot 1: The first study was undertaken with six classroom professionals who had a variety of responsibilities in a large children's centre in England. A case study approach was used at an individual and institutional level to explore both the children's centre and its arrangements for professional development and individual staff participation in the research. Meetings with the participants who had agreed to use the process model were held on a monthly basis to discuss their progress and semi-structured interviews with the Centre Management Team, who were responsible for the professional development of the staff, were held at the beginning of the process. The participants kept a formal record of the process, which they submitted at every meeting and they also retained a personal log of the process, which they used to discuss their experiences.

Pilot 2: The second study was undertaken with six secondary school teachers in a college catering for a full range (age and academic ability) of students in the Netherlands. The data collection process was similar to Project 1. In addition, in-depth interviews were held with school leaders during each visit to ensure clarity in our understanding of the professional development policies and practices of the schools, to induct the management team into the model and the process and to provide regular updates on the research.

Pilot 3: The third study was undertaken with five teachers in a special primary school (catering for children with a range of educational needs) in the Netherlands. The data collection process was the same as that undertaken in Project 2.

Pilot 4: Document analysis of eight applications by providers of professional development for recognition of good practice by the PDB-PE using the revised process was undertaken. A group of 22 providers also attended a workshop where they used the final version of the process model and provided feedback.

DEVELOPING THE MODEL

An important part of the process of developing the model was a review of recent and current literature and research about measuring impact, as discussed in Chapters 5 and 6. Two issues stand out in an examination of this literature, planning for impact and the involvement of pupils in the process, if it is to be effective. The need to begin the process of selecting teacher professional development with the child and the importance of impact are current topics of important

interest and concern in education in England and internationally. Planning for impact at the outset of a professional development activity has been recognised as important by some professional development providers (TDA, 2009) and rather than the measurement of impact being regarded as a concluding activity this expectation is built into the programme from the start. Notions such as "putting children at the heart of all that happens" (Ofsted, 2008, p.5); *Being the best for our children* (DCSF, 2008); and putting "student learning at the heart of all professional learning" (Cordingley, 2008, p.26) are clearly embedded in current literature, reports and policy.

Several models have been produced to describe a process which attempts to measure the effectiveness of professional development experiences and Guskey's (2000) model of five levels of professional development evaluation is probably the most well known. It was originally developed by Donald Kirkpatrick to assist professional development providers to evaluate their provision and was developed further by Guskey. The original model had four levels:

1. Participants' reactions
2. Participants' learning
3. Participants' use of new knowledge and skills
4. Student learning outcomes

This list will be familiar to anyone who has attended a professional development event and has been asked to complete an evaluation at the end of the day. Unfortunately, levels two to four are rarely addressed by providers when evaluating the impact of professional development and an assumption is made that these levels automatically follow on from simply attending a professional development event.

Guskey added a middle level, 'organisation support and change' because he found that unless there was support within the participants' schools and the intention to make changes, the professional development would not have the desired impact. He subsequently found that educators are exploring a reversal of the model, i.e. starting with student learning outcomes and how they will be assessed, then asking what new knowledge or skills are needed, and then getting the support of the organisation to participate in the development activities (Kreider & Bouffard, 2006).

This model is clearly very useful but the focus remains on individual action and development and does not recognise the importance of context and culture on the success of the process. The level Guskey inserted in the middle of his model is, we believe, best situated as an underpinning assumption and this was our starting point for the development of the process model. If the organisation, school and department, in which an education professional works are not supportive and have not embraced a culture of continuous review, change will not be possible and the rest of the process will break down. Such a structure requires an holistic approach to professional development with recognition that national, institutional and individual needs are taken into account in the planning of professional development activities. Cordingley (2008) suggests that the key benefits of aligning staff professional development with school, departmental and individual priorities through the performance system are that

CPD becomes a clear means to an end

Professional learning is focused on and driven forward through the lens of pupil learning

Staff members are more confident and enthusiastic about their professional learning and more willing to take risks and open up their practice - partly as a result of the focus on pupil learning.

Collaborative learning creates a learning culture within the school. Each learning benefit experienced by a teacher is immediately fed back into learning benefits for pupils – and vice versa. (p.32)

In 2007, as a result of a *Best Evidence Synthesis Iteration* on teacher professional learning and development, using international literature but grounding the implications in the New Zealand context, Timperley et al., produced a 'teacher inquiry and knowledge building cycle to promote valued student outcomes'. It consists of five steps:

1. Identification of students learning needs
2. Identification of teacher learning needs
3. Design of tasks and experiences
4. Teaching actions
5. Evaluation of the impact of changed actions

These steps are similar to the stages we have included and piloted in our model. However, while they acknowledge the importance of an appropriate context for professional learning, we have included culture and leadership as a stage in the process model. We have also emphasised the importance of evidence identification, together with a clear understanding of how this may be gathered, at stage one, prior to the teachers' identification of their learning needs. Our model is also founded on an inclusive approach to learning and teaching, identification and assessment, as discussed in Chapters 3 and 6, and promotes the development of more inclusive practice. The requirement for reflective practice is also part of the context culture and a prior expectation of participants rather than being considered at stage 2. Professionals are required to look specifically at students' needs and to engage in the process on a daily basis as an integral part of their professional practice. Our final model also recognises the need for participants to retrace their steps within the process and to re-engage with professional learning where putting their learning into practice has resulted in the identification of further learning needs.

In the model we are proposing, education professionals do not select professional development activities in isolation and the activities themselves are not limited to a course; they are selected in collaboration with colleagues and line managers with the pupils' learning at the centre of the selection process and clear understanding of the evidence required to demonstrate that the proposed learning has been achieved. The model starts and ends with pupils' learning in a supportive environment within an organisational culture that is inclusive and clearly focused on enabling the professional learning of its staff. For this model to work there is an assumption that the school has embraced a culture of continuous self-review. The next section explores issues about the context and culture required for the adoption of this approach.

Context And Culture

Able teachers are not necessarily going to reach their potential in settings that do not provide appropriate support or sufficient challenge or reward (OECD, 2005, p.9)

Hodkinson (2009) emphasises the importance of context, suggesting that existing teacher development research does not deal fully with the significance of everyday working practices for teacher learning. We must consider the context and the culture in which education professionals operate to fully understand the challenges they face in trying to develop themselves.

In order to develop and to use their learning, education professionals must work in a supportive context and factors that influence teacher learning include leadership, organisation and allocation of resources (Scribner, 1999). An appropriate learning and development culture is vital if professional development is to make an impact (Law, 1999; Hargreaves, 1994; TDA, 2009) and professional learning must be embedded in the culture of the school (Scribner, 1999). Timperley et al., (2007) take the analysis further in their identification of seven elements in the professional learning context, which are seen as important in research in the area. They are

providing sufficient time for extended opportunities to learn and using the time effectively; engaging external expertise; focusing on engaging teachers in the learning process rather than being concerned about whether they volunteered or not; challenging problematic discourses; providing opportunities to interact in a community of professionals; ensuring content was consistent with wider policy trends; and in school-based initiatives, having leaders actively leading the professional learning opportunities. (p. xxvi)

While we would not disagree with any of these elements, and indeed we have included some of them in our own description of essential contextual elements, some of them require further clarification before they can be accepted as an essential element. For example, engaging external expertise, which they suggest is necessary but not sufficient, should not be an assumption for all professional development but should be based on consideration of learning needs.

While acknowledging that professional learning does not only take place in an institutional environment, the influence of the culture that education professionals encounter in their everyday practice should not be underestimated. Therefore, awareness of cultural implications by those who work in the classrooms and those who lead and manage the professional development process is important. As discussed in Chapter 2, the culture of a learning organisation is determined by the nature of the model of professionalism adopted by the individual members of the community. Hargreaves (1994) identifies four forms of teacher culture within schools, individualism, balkanisation, collaboration and contrived collegiality, which are useful in describing communities in learning organisations. Individualism reflects the culture in which many teachers operate, where isolation is forced through the closed classroom door and an unwillingness to share practice or to be seen in action. Inevitably a culture of individualism narrows professional learning opportunities and limits the sharing of expertise. However, promoting close collaborative learning over isolated, individualist working is not as straightforward as it appears; it is not always a problem to work alone and indeed it might be necessary sometimes and can lead to important independent and personalised learning. The promotion of professional learning communities, as discussed below, may be one way to allow for and value individualised and collaborative working. Unfortunately, one outcome of specialised learning communities is balkanisation, which often dominates in secondary schools and while commonly seen in the form of subject groupings it can also be identified in other types of learning centres where the staff are divided into clearly defined structures and most activity takes place in those groups. Groups are sometimes in competition for resources and the culture is rooted in the status and priority of the subject or group; they are seen to have a strong identity, work closely together and spend much of their time, including social time, together. Therefore, learning is often guided by group norms and expectations and the practice of adopting group beliefs is not questioned, which can be both limiting and unhelpful to the professional development of group members. A different form of group culture can be recognised where a democratic model of professionalism is adopted and staff work together to achieve group targets within a collaborative culture, however, this culture does not emerge automatically but has to be developed. The final form of culture, identified by Hargreaves (1994), contrived collegiality, is the result of enforced collaboration, for example, when individuals are forced to work together in imposed groupings. However, while this can be seen negatively, as stated above, it can also have positive outcomes and can assist teachers to move towards collaboration. Each of these cultures may be visible in any one institution and therefore an awareness of how their adoption has the potential to affect professional development and consequently pupils' learning is important. Successful adoption of the model presented in this book requires education professionals to work within a collaborative culture and we believe that professional learning communities may provide the context for such a culture to be developed.

Professional Learning Communities

The notion of professional learning communities is raised briefly in Chapter 4 in relation to a discussion about high quality professional development and how professional learning communities might contribute to ensuring that good practice is shared. The following section considers the same concept in relation to the culture of professional learning environments, with the belief that any examination of the learning community must consider education professionals' and pupils' learning, as addressed in Chapters 2 and 3.

The purpose of a professional learning community is to ensure that the culture of a learning organisation is focused on learning, however, Day and Qing Gu (2010) propose that a successful learning community also demonstrates 'collective efficacy', that is, the belief by the members in the success of the community. Related to this is the concept of 'academic optimism'. In a learning community where judgements are made about individual and collective achievements, it is important that education professionals demonstrate belief, not only in their ability to make a difference, but also in the children's ability to succeed. This issue was identified by Timperley et al., (2007) in a list of elements where the notion of 'challenging problematic discourses' was raised, i.e. teachers must believe in the potential of their pupils and not make assumptions based on labels. The adoption of the model, presented in this book, requires everyone involved in professional development processes to believe that they can improve children's learning and to engage in professional learning activities that will have a specific impact on children's learning.

Bolam et al., (2005) define a professional learning community using terms such as inclusion, shared learning vision and mutual support for a group of professionals who work and learn together to improve their practice. However, Wenger's (1998) analysis presents teacher learning in three interconnected and interdependent levels:

Individual – engaging in and contributing to the practices of the community.

Community – refining practice and ensuring new generations.

Organisations – sustaining interconnected communities of practice through which an organisation knows what it knows and becomes effective.

This analysis recognises the different functions and interests of individuals, as individuals, as members of a community and as members of the whole organisation. It also highlights the importance of sharing practice in order to ensure community progression and effectiveness. Fielding's (2006) analysis of the relation between functions and members emphasises the point made in Chapter 4 about the difference between a learning community and a learning organisation. In this analysis, a learning organisation may be effective but not necessarily 'instrumentally successful'. This highlights the difference between a community that has self-belief and has adopted transformative or democratic professionalism and an organization that has adopted a managerial approach to professionalism.

Naturally, while there are huge benefits in developing a professional learning community, it must also be recognised that the development of a community, as described above, is not an easy task and there are constraints on its effectiveness. Bowe et al., (2010) summarise these as, "a lack of agreed and explicit knowledge base; repressive power relations and distrust; the large investment of time required to develop common language and purpose; cultural norms of privacy; and collegial niceties that detract from critical analysis of practice" (p.3). Imposing a professional learning community is likely to result in these constraints becoming visible in practice, thus preventing progression to a genuine professional learning community. Imposition may lead to a highly effective organisation but may also result in a learning community, reminiscent of the culture of contrived collegiality mentioned above. Evetts (2003), in examining two sociological interpretations of professionalism, a normative value system and an ideology of occupational power, suggests that if professionalism is imposed on the professional group, the normative value of the concept of professionalism may be used as an ideological control instrument, a mechanism to promote and facilitate change. Where professionalism is driven from within the professional group, it constructs and controls the ideology resulting in the empowerment of the participants and is likely to result in the development of a learning community. Therefore the form of culture adopted by, or imposed on, a school or learning centre is crucial in ensuring that a professional learning community is achieved. It is the latter form of professional learning community where participants are empowered to take responsibility for the development of their learning community, sharing learning, supporting each other and focusing on children's learning that, we believe, will enable successful adoption of the model presented in this book.

Leadership

The leadership of an educational organisation is another important factor in determining the culture adopted by the individuals in a group and a leader has the power to affect pupils' learning and the professional learning of the staff. This is a particularly important factor in the successful adoption of the model and is discussed further in Chapter 9. However, although it is generally accepted that leadership is important in ensuring that professional development is effective (McCormick et al., 2008; Day & Qing Gu, 2010), it should also be recognised that while leadership can be highly instrumental in raising standards, it can also be negative depending on how it is implemented. Leaders who foster a collaborative culture also encourage professional development (Day, 2000; Novick, 1996). Clement and Vandeburghe (2001) present two examples of how the relationship between leader and staff affects professional development. In the first example, collegiality is the dominant culture and the leadership promotes varied and rich learning opportunities and in the second, leadership promotes situations where autonomy is expected and little interaction between staff takes place. Law (1999) identified four leadership determined cultures and found that in a collaborative culture, staff commitment to professional development was high and the leadership was collegial. Within a directive professional development culture, a bureaucratic approach meant that development was seen as 'jumping through hoops'. A complacent culture resulted in professional development being seen as a low priority and little leadership provided. Finally, an individualistic culture resulted in teachers having to drive their own professional development, taking a self-centred approach, with the nature of professional development in the school being unimaginative and unplanned.

The type of culture necessary for the model presented below to work is based on the adoption of democratic professionalism, where learning is at the heart of the institution and individual members of staff are encouraged, supported and facilitated by leaders to take control and responsibility for their professional learning in a collaborative professional learning community where members are critically reflective. The focus for learning and teaching is pupil centred and the outcomes are inclusive.

THE MODEL

The model proposed here is intended to make the link between the expectations that education professionals will take responsibility for their own professional development and that they will critically evaluate the impact of their professional learning and teaching on their pupils' learning, within an inclusive approach to practice. The model can be used in any context, where the type of enabling culture, identified above, is embedded. The questions provided within the guide we have designed are intended to support and facilitate users as they work through the process. In addition this model is underpinned by a conviction that the learning of staff and pupils is equally important and inextricably linked within the development process, unlike the situation in many schools or learning centres where the learning of staff is often regarded as secondary to the learning of pupils/students (Hodkinson, 2009).

The model has evolved through several stages to emerge as a cyclical process that accommodates a flexible approach to selecting professional development and recognises the potential need to retrace steps while engaging with the process. Initially the model was described diagrammatically as a linear process with a clear beginning and an end and an acknowledgement that an appropriate culture is absolutely necessary (Figure 3).

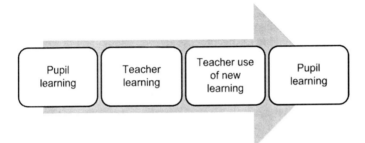

Figure 3. Model 1.

Following the first pilot, a second version of the model was developed which moved towards a cyclical process recognising the need for participants to revisit stages within the process while putting their new learning into practice. Participants of the pilot found that, having put their new learning into practice, that they needed further professional development in order to fully address the pupils' needs. Thus the diagram below (Figure 4) demonstrates how participants can move between professional development and implementation in practice several times in order to meet their learning needs and those of the children.

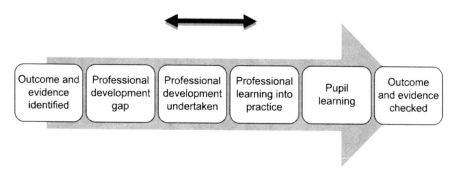

Figure 4. Model 2.

As a result of focus groups and discussions with education professionals we further developed the linear model to represent a cyclical approach, ensuring that the need to return to professional development mid cycle was retained. This revised model was then trialled in two further pilots and also with professional development providers.

In practice, this model recognises education professionals both as learners and as agents of change and requires them to be critically reflective practitioners who ask questions about their own practice and actively seek solutions and evidence of their success. It assumes the value of research and theoretical influence on teacher development and goes beyond a merely technicist approach to the learning of professional skills. It requires them to reflect while engaging in practice, to evaluate their practice and then to act to improve practice as a consequence of the process of reflection. Essential questions for education professionals to ask themselves at the beginning of this process are,

– How effective am I in my role?
– How do I know how effective I am?
– What evidence do I need to demonstrate effectiveness?
– Could I be more effective?
– What help do I need to meet identified needs?

The answers to these questions provide the preparation for engagement in the first stage of the process model. (See Figure 5)

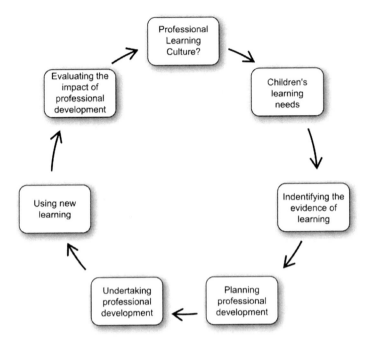

Figure 5. Model 3.

The model begins and ends with pupils' learning and to be effective must take place in a supportive environment within an organisation that is clearly focused on enabling the professional learning of its staff and motivating them to improve through setting their own targets rather than having them imposed, as discussed above. The first stage requires teachers to question their own effectiveness in relation to pupils' learning and to consider what evidence they would need to demonstrate effectiveness. They are then required to work with colleagues and line managers to identify development activities to improve effectiveness and then to participate in the professional development activities. Having participated in the development activities, and used their new learning with their pupils, they evaluate its effectiveness by gathering and interrogating the evidence, which they identified at the beginning of the process.

This model makes a clear and direct link between the demands made on teachers to take responsibility for their own professional development and the need to provide evidence of the impact of their professional development. Most importantly, if teachers are clear about what outcomes they are seeking and what evidence will demonstrate their effectiveness at the beginning of the process, there will be no need to seek data retrospectively or to rely on anecdotal evidence. The model also recognises and is based upon the characteristics of high quality professional development, as discussed in detail in Chapter 4. It has been suggested that it is difficult to control and to judge the effectiveness of randomised professional development, the suggestion being that only with specific professional development activities can this be achieved (Wayne et al., 2008). However, this model promotes a flexible and yet focused approach to the selection of professional development activities. The process ensures that selection of activities is not random, but is clearly linked to intended outcomes; these activities could be short term, e.g. one day courses, but if they are selected as part of the identification of needs relating to pupil learning they will be relevant and effective in practice.

Education professionals must work with colleagues and the school /centre management team to find appropriate professional development to meet clearly identified development needs and this must not only mean going on an external course or indeed merely learning from immediate colleagues, but must include a range of activities. A report by the General Teaching Council for England (GTCE) (2005) suggests that the most effective professional development occurs within collaborative activities and identifies teachers as key players in supporting and sustaining their own professional development and that of colleagues. However, while collaborative activities may provide sustainable professional development it is also important be aware of the dangers of being 'over-influenced' into accepting dominant group culture. This may happen in a small school community or in subject department and education professionals should work hard to avoid this.

While we acknowledge that some learning is unintentional and unplanned, if teachers are thinking and reflecting about their development and understanding the processes of development this will become an integral part of their way of working or learning. Those unplanned and unintentional learning episodes can then become part of a planned process because they are recognised as learning and subsequently evaluated as part of the reflective process. In fact, all engagement with the process should become part of a natural inclusive process where teaching and pupils' learning and professional learning are inextricably linked.

Using The Process Model

As part of the development of the model we found it important to provide a series of questions or prompt to support users through the process. This set of questions is not intended to be definitive, but it did provide participants in the pilot projects with guidance through the process, which they found to be helpful.

1) THE ORGANISATION'S LEARNING CULTURE
Developing reflective practice – engaging in a continuous process of
reflective practice Using a reflective log?

Questions to ask:
How effective am I in my role?
What am I good at?
What aspects of my role cause me difficulties?
How do I get professional development support?

2) THE CHILDREN'S LEARNING NEEDS
Being more effective.

Questions to ask:
What could I do to improve the children's learning?
How do I identify children's learning needs?
Do these strategies provide me with enough information to identify learning needs?
What do I need to learn, to know, do or understand in order to improve children's learning?

Task: Identify specific needs in relation to your work with the children – select a specific
focus for your learning, which relates to improving children's learning.

3) IDENTIFYING THE EVIDENCE OF LEARNING
Knowing I am more effective.

Questions to ask:
How will I know if my professional development is addressing the children's learning needs?
What evidence will I need to show that I have become more effective?
What would the children know, be able to do or understand if my professional
development has an impact on learning?

Task: Identify the specific evidence you will require to demonstrate evidence of impact
on children's learning

4) PLANNING YOUR PROFESSIONAL DEVELOPMENT

Questions to ask:
What professional development will I need to undertake?
Have I identified clear objectives in relation to children's learning?
Who will help me to meet these needs?
What help do I need to achieve these outcomes?

5) UNDERTAKING PROFESSIONAL DEVELOPMENT

Questions to ask:
What have I done to develop?
What or who has made it possible for me to develop?

6) USING NEW LEARNING WITH CHILDREN

Questions to ask:
How am I going to incorporate my own new learning?
How has my practice changed?

7) EVALUATING THE IMPACT OF NEW LEARNING

Questions to ask:
Has the children's learning improved as a result of my professional
development – how do I know?
Can I gather the evidence I identified in stage 3 of this process now I have
undertaken the professional development?

Figure 6. Using the process mode.

CHAPTER SUMMARY

This chapter has discussed the approaches used in the development of a process model designed to support education professionals to measure and provide evidence of the impact, of their professional development on pupils'/students' learning. It has focused specifically on the issue of culture and context, the elements of an effective learning community and the approach to leadership necessary to ensure that the model can be used effectively by education professionals. The development of the model has been discussed and the final model presented and explained. Employing the model requires a cyclical process through which participants engage in a course of action that will link their learning directly with the learning of their pupils but most importantly ensures that they identify the evidence, which will demonstrate impact, at the beginning of the process. Chapters 8, 9 and 10 draw on the experiences of the pilot groups to explore how the model can be used by different groups and in different contexts to address the needs of classroom professionals, leaders and managers and professional development providers.

SECTION 3

USING THE PROCESS MODEL

PRACTITIONERS

This chapter draws on the cases investigated through the pilot studies referred to in Chapter 7, in order to undertake a critical examination of how the process model presented in this book can be used by practitioners. The term practitioner is used to distinguish from the leaders and managers, who are the focus for Chapter 9, and the professional development providers, who are the focus in Chapter 10. A selection of case studies from the pilot studies provides examples of how the model has been used in practice and an overview of each stage of the process identifies the issues encountered by participants in using the model. This is followed by a summary of how the model may be used in practice and an acknowledgement of the benefits and limitations of the use of this model by practitioners. Throughout the chapter we consider the implications of adopting the model for practitioners providing learning experiences for a range of pupils in different age phases and/or with different subject specialisms in schools and learning centres.

THE PROCESS MODEL IN PRACTICE

The case studies presented throughout the chapter provide examples of how participants working in different contexts engaged with the process, the benefits they identified and the barriers they encountered as they worked through the stages of the model. The case study reports highlight how practitioners, working at different stages of the model and in different phases of education, encounter specific challenges. These case studies demonstrate that the process model has the potential to engage practitioners in reflective practice and to help them to consider the relationship between children's learning and their own professional development. There were many examples of how the process changed practitioners' approaches to learning and teaching, however, inevitably there were also several parts of the process that caused problems for the participants and this also helped us to refine our thinking about the model.

The following section uses the seven stages of the process model to identify and discuss issues specifically relating to practitioners. However, prior to this, an analysis of the reasons given by those practitioners who, at various stages of the pilot projects, withdrew, provides a valuable insight into the way they think about their professional roles, how they are supported to develop and how they deal with what could be seen as development conflicts.

In each pilot study there were participants who withdrew from the research, and while it was disappointing that some of them withdrew after the initial meeting and explanation, it is the participants who embarked on the process and withdrew at later stages in the research and the reasons they gave that are of particular interest.

CHAPTER 8

We were able to identify five reasons for withdrawal, the first three, which will be discussed in this chapter, are that engaging with the process model was too time consuming, or they experienced development conflicts or they encountered process difficulties as a result of the subject based organisation prevalent in secondary schools. The final two reasons given, school culture and perceived lack of support, are discussed in Chapter 9 as they relate closely to management and leadership issues.

---

[1]Lesley

Lesley was an early career teacher in a secondary school in The Netherlands who initially volunteered to participate in the pilot study as she was interested in the process and could see how it might support her professional development. She was clearly committed to improving her practice and was at that time participating in a part-time postgraduate programme. However, at our second meeting she stated that she did not feel she could carry on participating in the pilot. She described how using the model was making her think about her practice and how she had become really involved in the process and as a consequence was falling behind with her coursework for the postgraduate programme. There was clearly a conflict within the available professional development time for Lesley.

At the second meeting we did, however, discuss the model and the difficulties she had encountered in two of the stages. The first difficulty concerned assessing her effectiveness, which she found difficult. The second difficulty was in linking her learning with the pupils' learning needs and she spoke about making changes to her practice and trying new things, but she had not considered the impact of her learning on the learning of specific pupils. She attributed this to the fact that, while she reflected on her practice and made changes as a consequence, these changes always seemed to be with a new class and there was little opportunity to focus on the impact of changes to her practice or to gather evidence of improved pupil learning.

The process of engaging with the model was described, by several participants, as time consuming and for some this was sufficient reason to withdraw from the pilot. The people referred to here are not those who described development conflicts, but those who simply stated that they were too busy to use the process. This was possibly the most worrying reason for withdrawal given as it suggests that the basic premise on which the model has been developed, reflective practice, is not something that is part of their professional practice. Of more concern is that some of the participants claiming lack of time were professionals with many years of experience in teaching. Of course, it is possible that their withdrawal could be linked to a lack of ability to balance management responsibilities with teaching and learning responsibilities. However, another possibility is that they withdrew due to a reluctance to change practice or to devote time to a review of practice that they perceive to be successful.

The second reason given also links to time, but for these practitioners it was not development conflicting with other aspects of their roles but development conflicting with other development opportunities. For example, several participants were clearly committed to their professional development as they had shown a real interest in the process model and had started to use it, in some cases with very real success, but they encountered development conflict due to also being enrolled on part time certificated programmes. There were also two participants who had recently taken on new roles in their organisations and were struggling with the conflict between required learning for a new role and engaging with a process that, while relevant to their practice and had the potential to help them to meet their development needs, was also demanding that they review their practice and identify development needs in a different way.

The final reason given by participants for withdrawal related to teaching in a secondary school and was only signalled by one of the participants but, given the difficulties encountered by the group of teachers in the secondary school pilot, this does not appear to be an isolated issue. The teacher found that she struggled to link her learning with the pupils' learning because she had so many different classes during the week and this could well have been one of the reasons that other secondary participants struggled to use the process. This does not suggest that the model is not appropriate for use in secondary schools, but does imply that more guidance is required for practitioners in such organisations.

Stage 1: The Organisation's Learning Culture

Developing reflective practice – engaging in a continuous process of reflective practice Using a reflective log?   *Questions to ask:*   How effective am I in my role?   What am I good at?   What aspects of my role cause me difficulties?   How do I get professional development support?

While many of the issues relating to organisational learning culture are relevant to management and leadership and are addressed in Chapter 9, the aspects of culture covered in this chapter are clearly part of a wider concern about appropriate learning cultures and focus on how individual practitioners operate in their own organisations. The main issues relate to the question prompts for teachers about effectiveness and professional development support in this stage of the process model (see Figure 6, Chapter 7).

Maria

Maria had just been promoted and, while keen to engage with the process model, she was very anxious about participating in the pilot. Her new role (with a new line manager) might have caused some of this anxiety, however, throughout the pilot she was critical of herself and her practice and admitted to focusing on what she cannot do rather than what she can do. She also felt that colleagues and parents should answer questions about her effectiveness rather than being required to provide this information herself.

She started to use a notebook to make notes about the process but her reflections focused on what the children could not do rather than her part in the learning process. She was clearly challenged by the demands of her new role and was disappointed with the new set of children in her care as she felt that they were not sufficiently independent. This became the focus for her professional development as she struggled to come to terms with it and what she should do to support them.

We discussed the professional development she might access as her first thoughts were based on an expert type of professional knowledge (e.g. internet, books) and she had not considered learning collaboratively with colleagues or getting support from her line manager as acceptable modes of development.

In the final meeting we discussed the process model and its stages. She had chosen to return to an earlier stage to gain more professional development, as the initial activity had not met her learning needs. At this stage, she was very anxious that her learning was not having an immediate impact on the children and we discussed different aspects of professional development and the length of time that might be needed to embed learning in practice. Her choice of learning need was a long-term project and she became frustrated with the children's lack of progress and the fact that the final stage, gathering the evidence identified earlier in the process, was in her case taking a long time. She was concerned about this and found it an unfulfilling end to her engagement in the project.

The questions that asked about individual effectiveness were most challenging for the participants in the children's centre. This may have been a result of the professional preparation for the roles they were undertaking and/or possibly their perceptions of having relatively low status in the hierarchy of the organisation. In the process of going through these questions with the participants it was possible to gain an insight into the culture of the organisation and the professional confidence of the staff. For example, when asked about her effectiveness, Nicola focused on an activity, describing what she did rather than how she did it and the effectiveness of her actions. For Maria and Sasha it was seen as a question that others should answer and Maria stated that parents and colleagues should comment on her effectiveness. It seems that they were not able to, not prepared to, or did not have the confidence to, evaluate their own effectiveness; they relied on others to do this for them. As discussed in Chapter 2, this response to professional development is typical of a culture in which managerial professionalism is prevalent and practitioners such as those described here rely on external assessment rather than critically reflective practice. Their reluctance to engage with an evaluative process could also be attributed to a lack of engagement in critical reflection, but it could also be due to a lack of professional confidence and self-efficacy. However, as Scheerens et al., (2010) report, there appears to be a positive relationship between self-efficacy and student achievement and therefore this is an important issue to address through the process model. If education professionals do not consider student achievement as part of an evaluation of their own professional effectiveness, they will not benefit from the self confidence of knowing that their work is effective.

We found that engaging with the stages of the process model can encourage education professionals to adopt a different approach and gain confidence as a result. For example, initially, Gita found it difficult to evaluate her effectiveness due to a lack of confidence:

At first I was scared to answer the question... I had never really thought about my strengths... Other people can tell you what you're good at.

In subsequent meetings, however, she was able to address this issue and began to talk about her work in a more detailed and confident way.

There were also participants in the other pilots who struggled with the question of effectiveness, for example, Susan spoke about always looking at what went wrong in her sessions rather than what was successful. She was too self critical rather than critically evaluative, but as she progressed through the model, she appeared to gain confidence and was able to identify positive changes in her practice through the pupils' learning. Her revised approach was far more inclusive and as discussed in Chapters 3 and 6, placed the students at the centre of the education process, rather than concentrating on what she saw as her own poor practice.

Susan

Susan was an experienced teacher who willingly embraced the process model and its aims and talked openly about her professional reflections and development needs. At our second meeting she talked about always reflecting on the things that went wrong in her sessions, but through engagement with the model she was able to adopt a much more positive approach to her reflections. She identified small group work as a learning need for some of her pupils and sought support from the school coach and together they devised strategies to use with the pupils. She spoke about how these new approaches seemed to be working and how she and the coach will now move on to video her work so they can evaluate and assess what has been achieved and what more needs to be done.

The participants clearly wanted to make an impact on the learning of the children and in the case of those working in the children's centre, they spoke about wanting to make a greater contribution to the overall work of the Centre, but initially they did not have the confidence to identify their own strengths or feel confident that they could make an impact. The opportunity and indeed expectation that members of a professional community will contribute to its development is an important element of the culture necessary for successful use of the process model. As discussed in Chapter 7, individual and collective efficacy (Day & Qing Gu, 2010) are important if a learning community is to be successful. Several participants in the research expressed a desire to become more involved in the higher level planning side of the activities and the targets they identified within the pilot demonstrated their enthusiasm for playing a bigger part in planning the learning of the children.

In answering the question about accessing professional development support, the participants demonstrated a gap between policy and practice, which is examined in more detail in Chapter 9. Many of them identified support for their professional development through informal channels and spoke about accessing help from colleagues, some of whom they regarded as mentors. The official channels for accessing support, such as line managers, were only cited as sources of development support in the smallest institution in the pilot studies. In the larger institutions, participants found ways to access professional development support from people they respected, but who were not necessarily officially responsible for their professional learning. Access to, and a willingness to request support from, a line manager may not necessarily be attributed to problems with a management structure but may be related to the ready availability of a support network in larger institutions. In such organisations, it is possible to find the answers to development questions from experienced colleagues without having to approach a manager on an official basis. Most of the participants knew what the school/centre's systems for performance management were, although some were critical of how seriously they were used. However, when it came to accessing financial support or time allocation they were not as confident in their knowledge.

Stage 2: Children's Learning Needs

Being more effective.
Questions to ask:
What could I do to improve the children's learning?
How do I identify children's learning needs?
Do these strategies provide me with enough information to identify learning needs?
What do I need to learn, to know, do or understand in order to improve children's learning?

The questions that challenged participants to consider how they identify children's learning needs, and whether the strategies they use generated enough information, provided the impetus for them to review their assessment strategies. In particular, as discussed in Chapter 6, the need to move beyond standardised testing was recognised as an issue by the participants. These questions provoked discussion about assessing learning and participants appeared to have very broad views about how learning might be assessed, which were not limited by policy driven views of evidencing educational achievement through testing. The final question of the stage, which asks practitioners how they can improve children's learning did not present any major problems for the participants in any of the pilot studies, in fact, as will be discussed in stage 5, reducing the scope of the learning focus was the challenge. They appeared to know their students well, although, as identified earlier, for some secondary school teachers who teach many different classes in the week, with many different pupils, this did present a challenge.

One of the difficulties identified at this stage concerned the tendency to take a negative view and to focus on what the pupils cannot do, or even to blame them for their failure to learn. However, the process required participants to adopt an inclusive approach to their practice, which begins with the assessment of what children can do, rather than a negative approach, which focuses on what they cannot do. This positive approach to learning is not only relevant for children but is also important for education professionals to adopt and as we saw in Martin's case, it has the potential to involve children in directing and taking responsibility for their own learning. Martin, had worked towards involving children in the identification of their learning needs and by the end of the pilot was accessing professional development which would help him to support the pupils themselves to identify evidence of their learning at the beginning of the learning process. This type of consultation process is also described by Morgan (2009) and Williamson and Morgan (2009).

Martin

Martin was an experienced primary school teacher and he very quickly found that the process model could help him to improve the learning of his pupils. In the second meeting he was able to describe how he had used the model to increase the children's independence by involving them in setting their own learning targets. He identified professional development using the Internet and books, the school Orthopedagoog[2] and colleagues to find out about involving pupils in target setting for learning. He also worked collaboratively with a colleague to set up a new portfolio based project which involved pupils in goal setting for their learning and through this project was able to assess progress and provide evidence to show that the development was working. Goals were negotiated with the pupils who became more motivated and he cited evidence of meetings with them to plan their learning. In the third meeting he described how pupils had become involved in setting their own targets for independent study and were monitoring them themselves. He identified increased motivation and engagement from the pupils as a result of this development. Issues were arising from the children themselves about how they would know when they had achieved the targets they had negotiated for themselves. Tests were used but they did not sufficiently address the scope of the achievement and the whole issue of assessment and how to demonstrate evidence of achievement was now taxing not only Martin and his collaborative partner, but also the pupils themselves. He felt it was vitally important that the pupils should decide themselves what counts as evidence of achievement. His next task was to look for support, to provide this sort of feedback and he was accessing professional development from the Internet and books, but also, more importantly, through the collaborative teaching partnership. He spoke about the model as professionally enhancing and as a very useful tool and a process, which helped him to focus on his practice. The reflective approach was a process that was familiar to him in his every day work but he found that using the model sharpened his focus and made him put children's learning at the centre of his thinking about his professional development.

One of the primary school participants, Willem, also had a great deal of success using the model after he had approached the question of children's learning needs in a positive way, asking what the pupils *can* do. He worked through the model focusing on his interactions and relationship with one pupil who was displaying challenging behaviour which was disrupting the whole class. Using the process model helped him to focus on the learning needs of the pupil rather than on his behaviour and this led to opening up a discussion with the pupil about pupil and teacher limits. This open discussion, involving the child, focused on his learning and started with what the child could do rather than what he could not do, which enabled Willem to concentrate on his strengths and to utilise them in the classroom situation. This led to much better interaction for him, the child and eventually for a considerably improved learning environment for the whole class. Willem discussed and evaluated this with his coach and accessed professional development through this one to one coaching relationship.

Stage 3: Identifying Evidence of Learning

> Knowing I am more effective.
> *Questions to ask:*
> How will I know if my professional development is addressing the children's learning needs?
> What evidence will I need to show that I have become more effective?
> What would the children know, be able to do or understand if my professional development has an impact on learning?

Most participants struggled initially with the questions in this stage and some were really challenged by the task of identifying specific outcomes and tended to describe the process of collecting evidence rather than the evidence itself. Collecting evidence of children's learning at the end of the process provided a real sense of achievement for those participants who reached this stage. However, for some it became a frustrating experience as their new practice, which had changed as a result of their professional development, was slow to take effect in some cases and they were not able to collect evidence of their pupils' learning as quickly as they had anticipated. This issue does need to be highlighted to participants at the beginning of the process and relates to the initial identification of children's learning needs and their own professional development needs.

Stage 4: Planning Professional Development

> *Questions to ask:*
> What professional development will I need to undertake?
> Have I identified clear objectives in relation to children's learning?
> Who will help me to meet these needs?
> What help do I need to achieve these outcomes?

The participants who accessed support from a coach or a mentor, or a more experienced colleague, appeared to have had more success using the model than those who tried to plan their professional development in isolation. Here the collaborative nature of learning is, clearly, important to the success of the model. The questions attached to this stage indicate that identifying clear objectives for the development activities and accessing support are important elements of the process.

There was a tendency for some participants in the pilot studies to identify huge areas of learning when identifying and planning their professional development. These areas were inevitably difficult to address, difficult to put into practice and consequently made it very difficult to provide evidence of impact. In such huge areas it was challenging to identify specific evidence of children's learning and the specific professional development activity needed to change practice. We found that breaking down the learning needs of the children, and consequently the professional's learning needs, made the whole process more manageable and as described in Willem's case, led to successful application of new learning with one pupil, which eventually led to improved learning across the whole class.

Willem

Willem was a class teacher in a special primary school. When he initially engaged with the process model, he identified aggressive behaviour in the classroom as a barrier to pupils' learning and he recognised that he needed support to deal with this difficult situation. He was very honest in his assessment of his learning needs and in the early stages of the pilot he accessed some professional development through the coaching scheme in place in the school. During our second meeting, where he was still struggling with these challenges, we encouraged him to narrow his focus, which led him to go through the process model focusing on the needs of one pupil, with whom he was having particular problems. Starting with this more focused approach enabled Willem to engage with the model in a more meaningful way and he spoke about how it had focused his thinking on learning, the pupil's and his own, rather than behaviour.

For some participants this stage was the point where they withdrew from the process as they found it overwhelming, however, others, while finding it difficult overcame the problem by breaking down development needs into small steps of learning. As Cordingley et al., (2005) highlight, there is a need to reflect on the match between identified learning and the length of time required for the professional development in order to have realistic expectations. The scope of the development identified will impact on the type and length of time needed and therefore, as addressed below, will affect the implementation of new learning and how that learning impacts on practice.

Planning professional development within this process encouraged participants to really focus on the intended learning outcomes and therefore to select activities that matched their needs and several participants used a coach to advise on appropriate activities. A further benefit of using the process was that they accessed a broader range of learning activities, which meant they had access to different professional knowledge types. For example, rather than limiting professional development to courses and books, which are types of *expert* knowledge sources, they started to work with colleagues to apply their new learning, which linked *expert* knowledge and *craft* knowledge to become *pedagogical* knowledge. They also started to consider the quality of the learning experience and to take this into account as they planned further learning experiences.

Stage 5: Undertaking the Professional Development

> *Questions to ask:*
> What have I done to develop?
> What or who has made it possible for me to develop?

Discussions with participants about this stage provoked some very revealing responses in that many recognised that they often begin their professional development with this stage, that is, accessing learning activities because they are convenient or just interesting, with little thought about their needs or the learning needs of their pupils. One of the secondary school teachers spoke particularly openly about this, stating that he did not engage with the stages requiring him to evaluate his effectiveness or to consider the impact and evidence of his development, he just undertook professional development.

As discussed in Chapter 2, there was a lack of clarity amongst most participants concerning a definition of professional development and some had to be prompted to consider and include the learning they achieved while working as professional development. Most references to professional development were initially related to *expert* professional knowledge, e.g. information on the Internet or in books or attending courses. However, some participants did access support and development from other colleagues by observing, working alongside them and collaborating in new projects. Using the typology of professional knowledge, presented in Chapter 2, proved useful during this stage. In discussing the types of professional development participants were acquiring it was possible to help them to broaden their understanding of professional knowledge and prompt them to think about how they might extend their professional learning. For example, where accessing *expert* professional knowledge is the predominant form of professional development, applying new learning in the workplace may be challenging and, as a result, not used in the classroom. As discussed in Chapter 2, *craft* professional knowledge is equally restricting if not informed by some form of *expert* knowledge, research for example. The question, *What have I done to develop?*, prompted participants to think about different types of professional knowledge and the value of engaging in different forms of professional development.

As discussed above, new roles and the learning associated with them and other professional challenges negatively affected participation during the pilot studies and it is clear that these types of urgent role related and long-term professional development needs must be balanced with shorter-term pupil focused needs. It is also clear that a pupil/evidence based focus for professional development has the potential to incorporate the longer-term needs and indeed can clarify focus and outcomes. For example, for a professional working in a children's centre, gaining a professional qualification will help to develop practice, however, while a teacher undertaking a masters programme might be able to link her/his own learning with her/his pupils' learning through research, for example, in contrast, some masters programmes are purely academic and unrelated to professional practice. Both types of programme have a place and a value but it is difficult to undertake a full time job in an education institution and at the same time participate in a programme that is removed from the reality of the workplace. This raises questions about how professionals cope with the, often competing, demands of gaining an award, that is a long term project (e.g. degree, diploma, MA etc), and their daily professional development needs. This is also a question for leaders and managers and is discussed further in Chapter 9.

Stage 6: Using New Learning with Children

> *Questions to ask:*
> How am I going to incorporate my own new learning?
> How has my practice changed?

Putting new learning into practice is possibly the most exciting aspect of professional development, however, it is challenging and it can also be daunting to change our professional practice. These questions encouraged participants to really think about using new professional learning and this was the stage when participants became very engaged with the process as they began to recognise the links between the earlier stages of the process and what they were trying to achieve. So often professional development is undertaken without real consideration of why it is being undertaken, how consequent new learning can be put into practice or indeed if it is needed. The process model makes answering questions like this redundant because all the planning and identification of outcomes and intentions has been undertaken at the beginning and is a constant focus throughout. However, while this stage is exciting, it can also be extremely frustrating as some of our participants found. Having identified and undertaken their professional development, they found it was not sufficiently relevant to meet the children's learning needs. In the first pilot study, as discussed in Chapter 7, we revised the model to accommodate a return to further professional development after this stage in order to address these concerns. However, while the opportunity to return within the process to access more professional development is appropriate in some situations, it also encourages practitioners to really analyse their needs and how they might meet them in the early stages of the process in order not to waste time.

In Chapter 2 issues of personalising and contextualising professionals' learning are discussed, and the need to make learning relevant to individual needs, the pupils' and the professionals', is emphasised. Sometimes education professionals engage in exciting projects and learn a great deal but never put their new learning into practice because it was not relevant to their daily work. The value of using the process model with these sorts of projects and the need to personalise professional development was clearly illustrated in the first pilot study when several of the participants mentioned working on a funded project that the Centre had been engaged in for two years. They talked about how interesting it had been and what they had learnt but some of them said that they had found it difficult to put their new learning into practice. Learning in a vacuum, where professional development lacks obvious relevance to the daily professional context is exactly what this process model seeks to avoid. Participation in a large project such as this may mean that the targets were not fully linked to individual professional development needs but focused on the centre targets or indeed in this case on a Government target. It would have been possible to link this project with the process model making the connection between the professionals' learning and the needs of the children. In this way it would have been possible for the project and professional learning to have a more direct impact on practice and children's learning.

Stage 7: Evaluating the Impact of Professional Development

Questions to ask:
Has the children's learning improved as a result of my professional development – how do I know?
Can I gather the evidence I identified in stage 3 of this process now I have undertaken the professional development?

This final stage of the model requires users to return to the decisions made at the beginning of the process in order to determine, by gathering the evidence of learning identified in stage 3, whether the children's learning has improved as result of their professional development. In the pilot studies, for those who had identified manageable learning targets this was a relatively simple process, however, for some it became a source of discontent as they were unable to see the immediate impact of their professional development. This is not a surprise and did not indicate failure on the part of the practitioner, as Timperley et al., (2007, p.xxviii) suggest, "under most circumstances, an extended timeframe is needed for substantive learning to occur".

Alicia

Alicia was a crèche worker who, from our first meeting, had shown an interest in and understanding of the aims of the process model and was able to identify very quickly how she would be able to use it. She appeared to be confident and knowledgeable about her work, possibly due to her experience and her concern and interest in the children at the centre. Throughout the project she used a notebook and process record sheet to reflect on her practice and drew on these notes when we met to discuss her use of the model. She was the only participant in the first project who worked her way successfully through the seven stages of the model.

Alicia identified that the children needed more support to learn through play and this was an area where she felt that she needed to develop in order to meet their needs. Having very quickly identified the children's learning needs and her own professional development needs, she then found the identification of evidence of children's learning challenging. She described the process of collecting evidence rather than identifying the evidence itself. The professional development Alicia undertook involved meeting with a colleague, who was not her line-manager, but who she described as a mentor, discussing her needs and learning from this more experience colleague. She also used books and the Internet to access specific knowledge about types of play. She spoke about not being sure how to access resources for professional development and stated that without her mentor she would not have been able to undertake the development.

At the final meeting we discussed the relationship between the professional development she had undertaken and children's learning and she was able to describe the whole process very confidently. She had been able to identify that the children were more involved in play and that their learning had increased. She spoke about how the changes she had made to resources and materials had made significant differences to their play. However, it was not clear how she had measured this increase in learning and it is questionable whether she had actually identified the evidence well enough in stage 3 to identify progress. Early in the process we had discussed the difference between gathering evidence of learning and being able to assess learning through evidence and it became clear that this was still an aspect of the process that she had struggled with. However, she did use the process of identifying evidence to plan for learning through play and she believed that it would not be difficult to embed the process into her everyday practice, using the observation schedules in place in the Centre. She claimed that using the process had made planning and assessing more possible. Reflecting on the whole process, she stated that she had found the identification of evidence of learning the most difficult part but that she had enjoyed participating and had learned a lot.

The participants were very positive about having engaged in the process and referred to several aspects of their work where participation in the pilot studies had helped. Even Lesley, who withdrew from the pilot because it was requiring a different and demanding approach to teaching, was positive about it. For example, Alicia spoke about how using the process had made planning and assessing easier and Gita clearly became more confident and spoke about how gaining knowledge had raised her self-confidence. Willem found the model to be "extremely useful as a process which made me think about learning – the child's and mine".

CHAPTER SUMMARY

It is clear from a practitioner's point of view that to engage with this model is challenging and requires a flexible approach to professional development in a supportive environment. The pilot studies suggest that the role of mentor/coach is clearly beneficial in working through the process and should be available to all practitioners. Full engagement with the model requires an honest and critically reflective approach to understanding practice, participants need to adopt an inclusive, reflective and reflexive approach to learning, which is demanding and can be, initially, time consuming. While the model is progressive and clearly sets out seven stages of engagement, using it can be *messy* and at times require the user to retrace his/her steps to access more professional development and/or clarify learning outcomes. However, it clearly has the potential to raise confidence, personalise professional learning and expand understanding of and participation in professional development activities. Using the model can enable practitioners to take control of, and responsibility for, their development. The professional development activities chosen by practitioners are clearly based on and linked to the learning needs of their pupils. Most importantly, as several of the participants of the pilot studies pointed out, this process could and should be embedded in everyday practice. As demonstrated by some of the participants, involving children in the process of identifying their own learning needs and the evidence to show they have been achieved has the potential to further enhance the use of the process model and to develop a more inclusive approach to practice, as discussed in Chapters 3 and 4.

NOTES

[1]   All names have been changed to protect the identity of the participants.
[2]   An Orthopedagoog is a qualified Special Education professional.

CHAPTER 9

LEADERS AND MANAGERS

Leaders play an important role in determining the culture of a learning organisation and the ways in which education professionals working in that community are supported to facilitate the learning of the pupils. As discussed in Chapter 7, leadership can determine the culture of an organisation and consequently the professional development of its staff, with different approaches to leadership resulting in differing priorities and levels of support (Law, 1999). Over the last three decades, the expectations placed on teachers and other education professionals in England have grown and we have seen a considerable number of policy and funding changes, which have affected professional development opportunities for education professionals. The introduction of national policies and organisational target setting has also affected the professional development of education professionals. The devolution of funding to schools, for example, has placed increased emphasis on the role of school leaders and managers in the process of supporting teachers' learning needs while at the same time ensuring value for their investment. These changes and developments are not restricted to the UK and they can also be seen to be taking place in many other countries. Using the pilot case studies, described in Chapter 7, as a basis for discussion, this chapter examines the roles of leaders and managers, in schools and learning centres, in supporting professional development. In particular, it considers the culture and practice that will support education professionals to use the process model presented in this book, and highlights the dangers of leaders misusing the model.

LEADERS AND MANAGERS

In the interests of clarity, it is important to highlight that leaders and managers in schools, colleges and learning centres use different titles, for example, the person with overall responsibility for a school in England is likely to be called headteacher, however, in other countries s/he could be called principal or director. For simplicity, in this chapter we will refer to this role as the principal. However, it should also be recognised that in addition, to the principal, there will also be other staff, holding leadership and management positions who report to her/him and who use a broad range of terms to describe their roles. These roles may relate to responsibility for a subject, an age phase or an aspect of education such as the pastoral care of staff and pupils, but within their responsibilities, at different levels in the organisation, they are likely to have some responsibility for leading and managing the professional development of their staff.

The distinction between leadership and management, or administration as it is more commonly known in some countries, for example in the USA and Australia, is also important to acknowledge as it relates to the form of professionalism promoted by a principal and played out in the culture of the school or learning centre. While it is not our intention to embark on an extensive debate about the definitions of leadership and management, it is useful to acknowledge that it is generally accepted that while leadership relates to influence, values and vision, management refers to performance (Bush, 2003). A principal, who leads, will be concerned with strategy and using her/his position to influence staff, while a principal who only manages will merely be interested in making systems work. Adopting different forms of professionalism will influence the leadership and/or management style of the principal. For example, a principal favouring a managerial form of professionalism is more likely to be a manager than a leader, whose focus is on compliance, is bound by external regulation, is reactive in her/his responses and values efficiency. In contrast, within an organisation displaying democratic professionalism, it is more likely that a principal will be leading the staff with a clear vision of what the organisation should offer. This principal will also encourage other staff, who have additional responsibilities, to lead and not just to manage his/her vision but to contribute to it. Having said this, the necessity and importance of structures and systems, and ensuring that they meet the community's needs, is also important, as are the roles of those who manage the processes.

The importance of leadership and its relationship to effective professional development is highlighted in Chapter 7 (McCormick et al., 2008; Day & Qing Gu, 2010) and in introducing the model in the three pilot studies we found that it was important to involve not only the participants in the initial expectations of the process model, but also to involve the management team and line managers as all need a full understanding of the model and their part in the process. This was particularly evident in the first pilot study where the principal had selected the participants who were to be offered the opportunity to participate without the involvement of the respective line-managers. The lack of formal involvement of the line managers in the process initially impacted on its overall effectiveness, however, in individual conversations with two of the line managers it was clear that they were keen to become involved and were very supportive of staff, they simply did not understand their part in the process.

Hierarchical management structures were evident in two of the organisations in the pilot studies and the danger of roles becoming unclear and being misunderstood by those lower in the order in such structures was apparent. We are not suggesting that hierarchical structures in themselves are wrong, however, they can be problematic if they exist without a supportive environment. The culture of the organisation can clearly have an important impact on all aspects of professional development (Law, 1999) as discussed fully in Chapter 7. Another important issue relating to how hierarchical structures can affect relationships between staff with different levels of responsibility within an organisation became apparent within the pilot studies when one participant spoke about fear of the management team and how the staff sometimes felt unable therefore to make their needs known.

Inconsistent management practices across an organisation can cause problems for the staff being managed and can lead to inequity in how professional development is supported. Indeed, it presented challenges for some of the participants in two of the pilot studies, where professional development support appeared to depend on the line manager and the confidence and determination of the participant concerned. Where a member of staff had a line manager who took his/her professional development responsibilities seriously, performance management was linked to meeting development needs. However, where a line manager did not provide support for professional development individuals made their own arrangements with varying degrees of success, as discussed more fully in the case studies in Chapter 8. Different line-management practices within a context will affect the success of this process model and, as discussed later in this chapter, there is clearly a need for a whole institution, department or group focus on using the model.

In considering the roles of people who may participate in leading and managing professional development for other staff, it is important to recognise the roles of coach and mentor. In each of the pilot studies there was evidence that these roles were important to the success of the selection and implementation of professional learning activities. The one-to-one relationship appeared to be important to those who had accessed professional development in this way, as it was perceived to be supportive, enabling and non threatening. Although the participants used the specific terms coach or mentor, the way in which they described the relationship and the support provided did not suggest any great distinction between the two. Kennedy (2005) supports this lack of distinction between the two terms, but suggests that coaching is more skill based and that mentoring reflects professional friendship. The way in which the participants in the pilot studies used the coaching/mentoring relationship was certainly a combination of these two descriptions.

CULTURE AND CONTEXT

From the initial development of the process model we have seen the culture of an organisation as an enabling or restricting element and indeed this was one of the driving forces for us to develop a model which emphasised the need for a supportive environment. In Chapter 2 the relationship between the professionalism adopted by members of a learning community and the resulting culture is examined. This relationship and the importance of a supportive learning community were evident throughout the pilot studies, particularly so when examining reasons for withdrawing from the pilot or failure to make progress using the model. In one case, the participant engaged with the model up to the stage where she needed to consider what professional development was required and at this point she claimed that there was little point in going any further as she would not get the necessary support to enable her to undertake the development activity. This was a complex situation and the reasons for the perceived lack of support were complicated, nevertheless, here was a member of staff who did not believe that she had access to the necessary support to enable her to develop. Another case, in a different context, demonstrates how one participant became isolated, feeling that he had lost direction and as a consequence tried to deal with this lack of focus by himself rather than accessing support. There was a sense here that the approach to professionalism he had adopted, and which was possibly promoted within the school, was one of individualism (Hargreaves, 1994) and isolation with an unwillingness to share practice. He therefore struggled to engage with the process model, despite expressing an interest in it and recognising its potential.

As we have made clear throughout the book, the type of culture necessary for the model to work most effectively is based on the adoption of democratic professionalism, where learning is at the heart of the institution and individual members of staff take control and responsibility for their professional learning in a collaborative, critically reflective, professional learning community. The focus for learning is pupil centred and inclusive. In essence, a clear understanding by all involved and a commitment to pupil focused and pupil driven professional development for all staff is embedded in the culture of the institution. This pupil centred approach was particularly evident in the children's centre, used in the pilot studies, where there was a clear focus on the individual learning of each child. The real possibility, to embed the process model as everyday practice in such an appropriate culture was recognised and supported by several participants and this was summarised by Michael, when he commented that, "it's really just good practice".

Professional Learning Communities

The importance of professional learning communities has been raised throughout this book and confirmation of the necessity of a positive, reflective and developmental culture as a pre-requisite to enable the process model to work became apparent very quickly in each pilot study. Terms such as inclusive, shared learning vision and mutual support used by Bolam et al., (2005) to describe a professional learning community provide an indication of why, in some cases, the process model was not used successfully. Bowe et al., (2010) provide a useful summary of what they identify as a growing consensus of what makes a productive professional learning community. They suggest that shared values and vision, collective responsibility for student learning, reflection on practice and collaborative and individual inquiry are essential. We believe that these provide the essential elements for the context and culture in which our process model can be used most successfully.

The first two elements, shared values and vision and collective responsibility for student learning, emphasise the need for leaders in schools and centres, who wish to develop as professional learning communities, to ensure that all staff have the opportunity to contribute to the organisation's vision. Wenger (1998) talks about the community creating its own understanding of joint enterprise and the need to allow members to exert a level of control over the agenda, which means determining the focus for individual and collective professional development. The resulting culture should ensure that learning is at the heart of the organisation, for all pupils and staff and that, in order to achieve this aim, leaders should 'actively lead' the community (Timperley et al., 2007). The other elements concerning reflection on practice and collaborative and individual inquiry, relate closely to the first two, in that, in order to achieve a shared vision, individual members of a professional learning community must take responsibility for reflecting on their practice and collaborating with other members to determine and meet the jointly determined aims and goals of the community.

Kennedy highlights the value and potential of professional learning communities, at the same time however recognising criticisms, which have been levelled at them:

> It is argued that while communities of practice can potentially serve to perpetuate dominant discourses in an uncritical manner, under certain conditions they can also act as powerful sites of transformation, where the sum total of individual knowledge and experience is enhanced significantly through collective endeavour. (2005, p. 245)

A professional learning community has, then, the potential to support the professional development of its members, but, as suggested in Chapter 2, there is also the danger that it may become a balkanised (Hargreaves, 1994) community, through which development is restricted to dominant community norms and values if it there is insufficient critical reflexivity. However, a community, where leadership values and promotes the learning of staff and pupils, which aims at improving and transforming practice and where critical reflection and evaluation are employed as key elements of the process of development and change, has the potential to make a very positive impact.

Policy and Practice

Unsurprisingly, a policy versus practice debate arose regularly in our discussions with participants in the pilot studies and, as highlighted earlier in this chapter, line-management practices, the nature of the individual involved and the culture of the organisation all contributed to the debate. What is written in policy documentation, for example, concerning performance management and its link to professional development, may not actually be implemented in practice across an organisation and this was a finding in each of the pilot studies. While a professional development policy or structure was in place, participants admitted that not everyone used it and stated that professional support and development were sometimes difficult to access. This led to a range of coping strategies being developed by individuals, some of whom were more determined, and managed to circumvent systems and structures to access people and support they perceived as useful. However, for others, the barriers were too great and they were unable to access the support they needed. Where policy and practice did not match, different personal responses were elicited from individuals, so that some blamed the system for their inability to access appropriate professional development, while others identified their own poor communication of their professional development needs as the cause of the problem. In other instances, while on paper a clear system of professional development referral existed, as described in Chapter 8, some staff did not understand it or chose not to use it and worked outside the policy to select the support that they perceived matched their needs.

Legislative influence Legislation had an influence on the arrangements for professional development in each of the pilot studies and as they took place in different countries this manifested itself in a range of different ways. In the Netherlands the schools did not have their own professional development policies or plans but processes were in place to support staff and these were guided by statutory requirements and benefits. For example, the agreed competencies for professionals working in special education, laid down by the Dutch government, were used to assess and identify professional development needs in the primary school. In the secondary school a personnel manager had been appointed to oversee the legislative aspects of the professional development of the staff. Legislation and its relationship to job security and promotion clearly has an impact on professional development arrangements and also the approach and behaviour of staff in relation to their development and identification of their development needs.

Policies, planning and professional development support structures In the case of the children's centre there was a *Policy for Professional Support*, which stated why professional support is important, the aims of professional support sessions and how they should be undertaken. The other two schools, used in the pilot studies, did not have policies or specific plans for professional development, however, this is not to say that they did not plan the professional development for their staff or indeed that they did not have a support structure in place. They did, indeed, have systems in place, which ensured that staff were supported, both financially and in practice, to develop. In different ways, each organisation, in the pilot studies, had a structure that supported professional development. example, in one of the Dutch organisations, annual interviews take place with a student coordinator to discuss professional development and staff have access to the personnel manager at any time, to some of the senior staff and to the coach, who is part time, and has particular responsibility for new staff. Staff are expected to take responsibility for the professional development meetings and to determine their own agendas. New teachers are provided with an induction programme by the coach, a position, which is not commonplace in schools but is growing in popularity in The Netherlands. The new teachers have ten meetings in their first year of practice with the coach, they set targets and are observed and in their second year they attend peer group meetings. However, the relationship between institutional development plans and targets and the professional development planning for staff is unclear. How does the institutional plan and any professional development identified within it relate to individual development plans? Scheerens et al., (2010, p.199) also identified this as an issue and questioned "the extent to which professional development should be a 'stand alone' policy priority or be embedded in a broader set of school policy measures".

Performance management With regard to performance management, as suggested above, policy and practice, do not always match. The systems in place for evaluating staff performance and identifying development needs in the pilot institutions were varied and did not appear to be overly bureaucratic and, in fact, some participants spoke about professional development plans not being used constructively and not being taken seriously by line managers. This was also identified in research undertaken by Scheerens et al., (2010) where they found that the outcomes of appraisal were often not followed up with the identified professional development, which they regard as extremely problematic. They emphasise the importance of appraisal, feedback and follow up, for both teachers and schools. A relationship between performance management and a personalised approach to professional development has been promoted by the General Teaching Council of England (2007):

> Well constructed performance management processes can provide the bridge between indentifying individual learning and development needs, providing highly tuned learning and securing high impact for pupils. (p.1)

In one of the pilot study cases, described below, assessment, feedback and professional development were successfully drawn together in this way.

The Principal and her deputy assess the staff using observations, pupils' opinions and work produced in the classroom. Each member of staff has an annual interview at which feedback from the assessment is provided and the previous year's professional development and work is evaluated. Discussion takes place about professional development needs and this includes consideration of the pupils' learning needs. Individuals then determine their own professional development plan, which they submit for approval. The approval process balances individual and institutional needs.

Resources Despite the provision of different types of professional development, which included Government led initiatives, school events, subject and year events and individual learning activities, many staff in the pilot studies struggled to engage with professional development in a meaningful way. According to the policy and support arrangements in each pilot study, time and resources were available, however, they were not always accessed by the staff as intended and many participants were unsure about resource availability for professional development. For example, in one Dutch school every member of staff is allocated an allowance each year to support professional development and by law, all teaching staff are entitled to 10% of their workload to be allocated to professional development. It is difficult, therefore to understand why staff might struggle to access appropriate professional development. The answer may lie partly in the way they define professional development, what support they expect as part of this process and how they expect the resources to be allocated. For example, many of the participants defined resources as the finance to attend a development event and did not regard colleagues as a resource. Most referred to professional development support as being given the time to attend a development activity and did not recognise informal activities as opportunities to develop. In one pilot study, most of the participants were unsure about resource availability for professional development and they spoke about there being little opportunity for them to access resource to go on a course. There is clearly a need for practitioners to broaden their understanding of professional development and for leaders and managers to make support frameworks clear. Using a description from Timperley et al., (2007) of a supportive learning context, we can begin to identify the issues of concern. Time, support from external agencies where necessary, opportunities to engage in a variety and range of learning activities are all elements that were visible in the structures and practices of the organisations in the pilot studies. However, if we look at the final part of their description, which suggests the need for engagement with a supportive community of practice, we can start to see why some practitioners struggle to identify and plan their professional development. If the right culture is not in place, the available resource will not be used effectively.

Making time to engage in development activities is always a challenge, however it is the responsibility of leaders and managers to ensure that their staff have the necessary time to develop. This means not only time to participate in development that contributes to school targets but it also means that time to develop to meet children's learning needs and any additional development needs related to career or role requirements should also be allocated realistic time in order to avoid development conflict. We should be aware of those education professionals who, as demonstrated in these pilot studies, have the potential to make a huge contribution to the organisation but because of their commitment are struggling to meet all role demands. It is possible that if they are put under too much pressure, while trying to develop in new roles and/or undertake long term career development as well as develop their practice in relation to meeting children's needs, without support, they may leave the profession or revert to doing the minimum to survive. This claim is supported by evidence from international research (National Union of Teachers (NUT), 2003; Gore et al., 2006; McCormack et al., 2004; Ingersoll, 2001; Strong & St John, 2005), which examines why teachers leave the profession. The research cites low salaries, lack of professional development opportunities, excessive administration, government initiatives and unacceptable student behaviour as teachers' main reasons for leaving the profession. Apart from low salaries, each of these issues has a close relationship to professional development and the time available, or unavailable, to develop professionally.

There were several additional resource challenges for managers, which emerged through the pilot studies, that we believe using the model can address. The first of these is a more equitable distribution of funding for professional development; in two of the pilot studies the participants were not convinced that this was the case in their institution. It should be noted that these were, however, perceptions and not necessarily reality, nevertheless the issue is still a problem. For example, where there is a legal requirement for all staff to be provided with professional development, access to support can be provided in a range of different ways and it is possible that individuals might not recognise elements of support provided as professional development. Funding for professional development may not be used or provided in line with how some individuals define professional development or identify their needs. For example, if they define professional development as going on a course and they are not given the funding for such learning activities they may feel aggrieved and consider that they have not been given access to professional development. Addressing this issue as a leader does not mean ensuring that all staff have access to the same financial resources, it means ensuring that all staff understand the range and variety of professional development possibilities and are provided with access to the development identified as necessary to support them to improve children's learning. An open and clear policy for professional development is also necessary as is a process for accessing support for professional development activities, which is transparent, understood by all and implemented in practice. We believe that the process model, presented in this book, has an important role to play in developing understanding about all these issues relating to access to professional development and supporting leaders in the development and implementation of transparent, just and equitable policies and practices in the area.

A second challenge relates to the need for a leader/manager to know the strengths of the staff within her/his organisation, in order to facilitate and support judgments about appropriate professional development choices for individuals and the allocation of resources to support those choices. Support from more experienced colleagues with specific strengths or expertise was the way several of the participants in the pilot studies accessed professional development, however, this arrangement did not always occur as a result of a planned organisational approach. This meant that unless a member of staff knew where to access support from her/his colleagues, she/he was not able to access appropriate professional development easily. It is therefore important for an organisation to have a clear understanding of its expertise it terms of staffing in order to make judgments about professional development support.

A third challenge is the requirement to take professional development plans and identified needs seriously. Using the model provides a clear process through which staff can assess their needs and justify the support activities necessary to meet them. If, as we have suggested throughout this book, a supportive, collaborative professional development culture is in place and there is strong enabling leadership, the model can be used very effectively to make the direct link between children's learning and professional learning and, most importantly, evidence of the impact of the professional learning will be provided. Thus the model provides leaders with a useful and developmental accountability strategy for the allocation of resources, which at the same time makes clear that the professional needs of staff are taken seriously and addressed. It should be noted that here the term accountability is being used in a developmental, supportive sense and not as a means to control, limit or manipulate professional development, a danger of which we are well aware and which is discussed further below.

Leaders and Managers Using the Model

It became clear through discussions with leaders and managers, in the pilot studies and within the focus groups, that they are often a group that misses out on substantial professional development. There appears to be an assumption that education professionals in leadership and management positions have already received the professional development they need to achieve this status and that any development activities they undertake are externally provided and linked to their leadership/management role. These may include for example, updates on policy, subjects or possibly a management course when initially appointed. This can be seen as problematic since a leader in this position is not setting a good example for his/her staff by confining professional development to these restricted opportunities and activities. During the pilot studies we found that the process model can be used by leaders as well as practitioners to assist them to maintain a focus on children's learning when they are thinking about their own professional development needs, as exemplified in the case study below.

> One of the principals in the pilots decided that she would work through the process herself, and she adapted the model to match her position and role expectations. She used the model to focus on her responsibilities towards her staff and pupils. She initially used it to help her to identify the developmental and learning needs of a member of staff who was having some problems with her professional practice. Working through the model she soon identified the need to focus on the pupils and their learning needs, rather than on the staff member. Using the model and focusing on the learning needs of the children enabled the principal to move forward with the problem. The focus on 'being a professional in the classroom' was an important part of working through the model as that, coupled with the focus on the pupils' learning, made clear the real issues relating to this staff member and helped the principal to identify the areas where the staff member required support. In order to address the issues identified she then sought professional development for herself and found a way to deal with them.

Why Would Leaders Use the Model?

Using the findings of the pilot studies, focus groups, interviews and discussions carried out during the development of the model it is possible to identify why leaders and managers may choose to use the model with their staff. The leaders we interviewed could see the potential in deploying the model with their staff and were keen for us to pilot it in their organisations. However, the potential they identified cannot only be viewed positively but can also be viewed, from our point of view, negatively. As stated at the beginning of this book, we are working in a period of high expectation in terms of performance management and value for money, and while it is certainly not the main aim of the process model, it could be used to help staff to identify appropriate and relevant professional development and therefore assist with both of these issues. Linked to this is the need for leaders and managers, as a result of devolved, increasingly diminished, budgets, to be accountable for the funding they use for professional development in terms of institutional outcomes and impact on student learning in terms of test results. This issue is often addressed by tying professional development to school targets and government targets, unlike this model, which ties professional development activity and outcomes directly with children's learning targets.

The management team in one of the schools in the pilot studies, also saw potential for using the model to motivate staff, citing lack of confidence to make professional changes in some staff as a problem. They spoke about using the model to promote effectiveness and while in this case it was seen in a developmental way, in the wrong hands, it could also be seen negatively and used to hold staff to account in a controlling fashion. We have been very clear about our motivation for developing this model and we are keen to avoid its misuse. For example,, in relation to control, in a culture where democratic professionalism is promoted, we believe the model could, and indeed should, be used to encourage self-regulation and self evaluation of professional development. In stark contrast, in a culture of managerial professionalism, the model could, of course, be used to externally regulate and control professional development an approach, which we would not support at all.

Another aspect of this discussion relates to the need to be accountable for any professional development we undertake, which can also be seen positively and negatively. There is no doubt that education professionals should be held accountable for any investment in their development and this has been a weakness in the past. Participants in the pilot studies spoke of situations where professional development activities had been selected randomly, with little reference to personal, institutional or, possibly more importantly, pupils' needs. The model helps to address this issue, as it requires individuals to focus on and select professional development, which is directly related to children's learning. The model is intended to develop the link between children's learning and professional learning and to help answer questions about impact, however, an application of the model, which holds people rigidly to account and limits professional development, is most certainly not the intention.

CHAPTER SUMMARY

The diagram below summarises how the model may be used by leaders and managers to reflect on their roles within the process

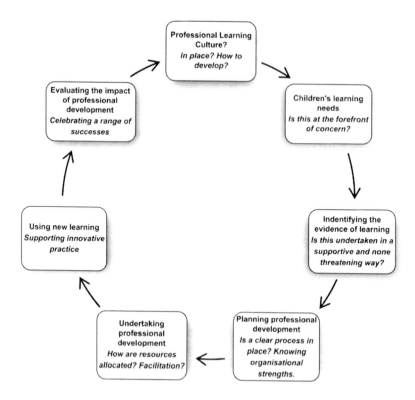

Figure 7. Leaders using the model.

   To be used successfully, the process model has several contextual and cultural prerequisites, which leaders and managers have responsibility for implementing. The culture of an organisation must be developed to achieve a collective vision, which focuses on the improvement of learning for both staff and pupils within an inclusive approach to practice. As stated throughout the book, a critically reflective approach to practice must be an expectation of all staff in the school/centre, however, leaders and managers must ensure that this is linked to strategic, explicit and transparent performance management and professional development planning. Planning for professional development should be clearly visible throughout the organisation, and whether a professional development policy exists separately from the school/centre targets or not, it should be visible and very much a part of the planning process. Above all, policy and practice should match. Individual professional development planning for staff should be part of this overall process and time and resources allocated, transparently, to supporting learning needs.
   From a leader's or manager's point of view, the model has the potential to enhance the organisation as a learning community. However, introducing the model into a school or learning centre should be a group enterprise and involve either the whole school or discrete sections of it in order for it to meet its potential.

For example, in a secondary school, members of a subject department could work together to adopt the model where a learning community is already in place, with a leader who has responsibility for the professional development of its members. The model is intended to make professional development planning realistic and to link the selection of development activities directly to children's learning and to demonstrate impact. Using the model to select professional development has the potential to contribute to a more equitable allocation of resources as all activities are justified in relation to intended impact and demonstrated by evidence. The model also encourages the identification and use of existing resources within the organisation, by using experienced practitioners to provide professional learning support rather than engaging and paying for external expertise where it is not necessary. It also has the potential to ensure that professional development is taken seriously and that performance management is developmental and supportive, includes assessment, feedback, identification of needs and access to professional development.

PROFESSIONAL DEVELOPMENT PROVIDERS

This chapter focuses on the ever expanding group of professional development providers which may include, amongst others, consultants, commercial businesses, LAs, colleges of further education, HEIs and subject associations. It will draw specifically on research undertaken with a range of such providers in England, which was commissioned by the subject association for physical education in the UK, afPE, to illustrate the need for serious consideration of the evaluation of the impact of their provision, not only on the participants of the professional development provision, but also on the 'end-users', their pupils/students. It discusses how the research inspired and informed the development of the process model presented in this book and provides an overview of how using the model to assist them to develop, deliver and evaluate their provision can support and enable professional development providers to meet the learning needs of participants more effectively, identify impact on their pupils/students and gather evidence to demonstrate that impact. At the same time by applying the model to the design, implementation and evaluation of their provision, providers are encouraged to place emphasis on the importance of gathering evidence to demonstrate and assure the quality of their provision.

THE PROVIDERS

Throughout this book, continual reference has been made to the wide variety of professional development currently available to education professionals and also to the increasing range of providers. This has come about as a result of changes to planning, organisation and funding of professional development. In England, funding available to access professional development in education is now devolved, for the most part, to schools/institutions, which make decisions about how, where and to whom it should be allocated. Government funding for the provision of professional development is allocated through an open, competitive bidding process, which has led to a range of private providers accessing funding alongside the more traditional providers such as HEIs and Local Authorities. Leaton Gray (2005) sums up the implications of this policy for schools and teachers. "Consequently, over the last seven years, schools have become increasingly reliant upon a range of providers for CPD, in a largely unregulated free market." (p.15). She cites as examples, not-for-profit organisations, museums, theatres, galleries and professional subject associations. In addition to these she points out: "There is also a thriving commercial sector of organisations such as private consultancies, research organisations and examining boards, which specialise in high-cost, high-profile training for teachers, offering both in-house and external provision." (op.cit.p.16). The same range and variety of providers can also be seen to be making professional development available to the wider category of education professionals, as defined in Chapter 1. Inevitably the adoption of an unregulated free market approach and the subsequently increased number of operators in that market has considerable implications for the quality and indeed the quality assurance of provision, issues which are addressed in considerable detail in Chapters 4, 5 and 6. Similarly devolving funding for professional development to schools/institutions has impacted considerably on the choices and the type and quality of provision available to education professionals, issues which are also discussed in much more detail in Chapters 2 - 6. Leaton Gray (2005) concludes: "In the best cases, a free market in CPD allows for a creative, entrepreneurial approach from providers, responsive to the needs of customers. However all too often, resources are wasted on poor or indifferent provision." (op. cit. p.29)

The central focus of this chapter, as indicated above, is to discuss the relevance and application of the process model, presented in this book and discussed in detail in Chapter 7, for this diverse group. Before moving to an examination of the application of the process model for providers, however, it is important to note that the development of the process model was informed, and to some extent inspired, by the findings of research carried out with a range and variety of professional development providers and this is why, we believe, it has great potential for use as a tool by providers in the development, implementation and evaluation of their provision.

The Role of Providers in the Development of the Process Model

As mentioned above, some subject associations in England have developed as providers of professional development for education professionals. In addition, they have also taken on an increasingly important role in the development of procedures to assure the quality of professional development provision. The subject association for Physical Education in the UK, afPE, has taken a lead in this work in recent years and through its Professional Development Board (PDB-PE) has developed a self initiated, self assessment process for quality assurance for providers and provision in the subject area. Using the PDB-PE's evidence based process of self evaluation against categories of quality criteria, providers are encouraged to apply for recognition for themselves, their provision and the resources and materials they develop and use. Applications are scrutinised by the Board and recognition is granted, subject to an ongoing process of updating and continuing self assessment. This process was developed in order to

– raise awareness amongst providers of the need to strive towards increasingly high quality provision;

- provide a bench mark against which the quality of providers and provision can be measured;
- provide a guide for professionals who want to access learning and development in the subject area to steer them towards high quality provision and providers.

As mentioned above the whole process is evidence based and applicants are required to identify and produce evidence to support their claims about their provision in relation to the aims, values and underpinning philosophy; management structures and personnel; accountability strategies and processes; management processes and outcomes and impact. This process was developed, trialled and evaluated with a range and variety of professional development providers over a period of three years, 2005-2008, by means of a longitudinal research project (Keay & Lloyd 2008).

While they welcomed the process and found it to be extremely valuable, throughout the research which led to the implementation of the, now established, process of application, providers involved raised many concerns about impact and evidence. They recognised the importance of impact and of providing evidence of impact but there was a lack of clarity regarding what is meant by impact; to whom and to what impact relates; how to demonstrate that it has taken place; what counts as evidence; how and when to collect it and who should collect it. This lack of clarity was evident throughout the discussions, which took place during the interviews with providers in the research, and was a key issue raised in the findings.

Strategies currently used to measure impact include:

- baseline assessment
- comparison of participant attendance at courses
- phone calls or follow up visits to the workplace
- case studies or success stories

There was a general feeling that insufficient was being done to identify the impact on the learning of the participants and that even less was done to identify the impact on the learning of the end-users. All were satisfied that the participants in the provision were feeding back that the experiences were positive, evidence from one provider being that *'all our courses get 1 or 2 rating on the evaluations forms'*, and yet they all felt that the forms alone were an unreliable indicator of genuine impact or indeed quality." (Keay & Lloyd, 2008a, p. 20)

As a result of the findings some recommendations were made to support and enable providers to address their concerns with regard to these areas. These included

- that the PDB-PE should gather exemplar case studies of 'good' practice in the area to be disseminated amongst providers;
- the development of a 'buddy' system so that providers could support each other with their self evaluation processes;
- the PDB-PE should provide workshops to support the application process.

In addition to these strategies particular recommendations were made in relation to the recurring issues of impact and evidence. "Unfortunately it is clear that this is an area where all CPD providers continue to struggle and we recommend that the PDB-PE considers looking at this as a specific issue in order to support providers." (op.cit. p.23). The specific recommendations to the Board were that

– the importance of the pupil/students as stakeholders of provision should be emphasised and recognised in the process of application.
– outcomes and impact should be more closely considered in relation to children's learning.

These findings and recommendations made to the PDB-PE in relation to the process of application for recognition had major implications for the development of the process model presented in this book. Discussions with providers during this research around quality assurance processes clearly highlighted a number of other major concerns with regard to the provision and delivery of professional development, all of which led back to the learning needs of the end-users of the provision, the pupils/students, and how to ensure that they are addressed. They also revealed that providers of professional development felt insecure and lacked support in the area of making effective links between provision, professional learning outcomes of the participants of their provision and pupils'/students' learning outcomes.

Timperley et al., (2007), in their wide ranging, international synthesis of best evidence in the area of professional learning and development, found that:

Few studies provided descriptions of the professional development, evidence of teacher learning and change, and student outcomes.... Another major problem was reporting student outcomes. This reporting was inconsistent and in many cases failed to reach even basic standards of adequacy. (p.xiv).

As a result of the research described above, it became clear to us that in order for questions about evidence and impact to be addressed effectively by providers it is necessary to shift the focus from the provision and even from the participants in the provision, onto the end users of the provision and their learning and learning needs, which as mentioned above, was identified as a major recommendation of the research. It remains vitally important, of course, that providers are concerned with the content, format, delivery processes of the provision and also with the experience of the participants and their learning needs and desired outcomes. However, retaining a focus on the learning needs of the end users and raising questions about how the provision is intended to impact on their learning, what evidence will be required to demonstrate that impact and when and how it will be collected, throughout the development, implementation and evaluation of provision, can enable both providers and participants to ensure greater relevance and appropriateness in all aspects. The research identified that this approach was lacking for many providers altogether and was, as above, a focus with which they struggled even when it was present.

The Process Model as a Tool to Support Providers

The underpinning theoretical justification and the organic process of developing the model are addressed in detail in Chapter 7. The research discussed above and the findings and outcomes contributed considerably to that process of development as they revealed a need for support for providers as well as education professionals which enables them to understand about impact and evidence and their importance. This inspired us to design and develop a resource to address this need. The process model places the focus on the learning of the end users, the pupils/students, in addition to the learning of the participants, the education professionals, and is intended also to highlight the importance of this focus for the professional development provision. The emphasis on identifying evidence of impact of the learning of the education professionals on the pupils/students has major implications for what form professional development takes and how it is delivered and this in turn inevitably has far reaching implications for the providers. As explained in detail in Chapter 7 the model requires a supportive learning culture within which education professionals

- are able to focus on identifying the learning needs of the pupils/students and what evidence will be necessary to demonstrate that those learning needs have been addressed;
- evaluate and assess their own learning needs in relation to those of their pupils/students;
- access appropriate and relevant professional learning and development;
- translate that learning effectively into practice;
- evaluate, and demonstrate through the evidence collected, the impact of that learning on the pupils'/students' learning providing feedback for further learning and development (pupils/students and education professionals)

It also requires that professional development provision enables and supports these processes and is designed to contribute to that learning culture.

Education professionals working through the model and identifying their own learning needs in relation to those of their pupils/students, then need to be able to find appropriate and relevant professional development to enable them to meet those learning needs. Clearly for them to have access to relevant and appropriate development and learning opportunities, which will support them as they implement the model, it is essential that the provision they access is relevant to, recognises and addresses their learning needs, but is also focussed on the identified learning needs of their pupils/students if it is to be effective. Issues relating to impact, what counts as evidence of impact and how and when to collect it, should also be an integral focus of the provision. The model can be seen to depend, for its success, upon providers being aware of and focussing on these issues when they design, develop, deliver and evaluate their provision.

Evidence and Impact

An analysis of applications for PDB-PE recognition, using the process described earlier, from a cross section of providers reveals, however, a number of continuing problems with what counts as evidence resulting in the evidence column in many applications being left completely blank. Where evidence is cited it is often intangible and anecdotal. Similarly, impact of provision is discussed, for the most part, in relation to the participants of the professional development and rarely in relation to the end users of the provision and where it is there is failure in this section also to identify evidence to support the discussion. Evidence of impact cited includes, for example; feedback forms; a reference from the school; general comments from pupils about how they enjoyed the lessons more; success stories; news stories on the website; workshop evaluation forms. One applicant states, very honestly, that

> A number of teachers report that provision has improved their teaching abilities and altered the way some teachers teach, but it is very difficult to measure the impact on teaching and learning on the pupils and is something we hope to venture towards in the coming year or so.

However, for a small number of providers, working with the evidence based process of application has certainly raised awareness about the importance of providing evidence of impact and it is an issue which they are beginning to address with some exciting strategies. One provider states

> Evidencing impact is something we are continuing to focus on. Our plans for 09-11 clearly demonstrate a shift from one off courses which have little impact on pupils' standards to a more longitudinal approach, once staff return to school, as there is little time currently given to reflection and support is distant. All programmes.... aim to offer follow up support, but more importantly all endeavour to encourage and develop those attending as reflective practitioners who are using their learning as a way of informing future practice.

This provider has also implemented the idea of impact evaluation reports where participants are required to reflect on and evaluate the impact of their learning, on themselves and on their pupils/students. Citing an example of impact of whole school, tailored to need, professional development the same provider states

> The sensitive and practical support offered to an infant school has resulted in a number of benefits. It has improved progress within lessons and across the school, increased professional dialogue and reflection in relation to learning, helped teachers to identify their own starting points based on pupils' needs and, more recently, led to teachers recognising that some form of tracking of individual progress will be required. The real benefits will accrue later because the Headteacher knows this is the start of a much longer 'journey'.

Clearly this provider has developed, and continues to develop, provision which is flexible, addresses the identified needs of the participants and of their pupils and which incorporates and supports the collection of evidence of impact on pupils within its design. Another, while recognising its importance uses more anecdotal evidence to support claims of impact:

> We have also measured impact of the professional development we offer by gauging the feedback from teachers who have used it and the activities in PE lessons.... There has been an obvious increase in enthusiasm and appetite for PE from both teachers and children, with one school noting an increase in their children joining physical activity clubs after school.

While this is, of course, an extremely small scale survey it is interesting to note that all applicants have addressed the issue of impact with examples of numerous strategies they use to assess it, as required by the process. These include peer observation, observing practice, follow up meetings, case studies, reports, email feedback and evaluation forms. Most of these strategies, however, continue to relate to impact on the participants and very few refer to the end users.

Using the Process Model with Providers

During 2010 a workshop was offered, by the PDB-PE, to address some of the concerns being expressed by providers about evidence and impact and to support them with the application process. Twenty-two providers attended, including LAs, private companies, individual consultants and advisory services. We used this workshop as an opportunity to trial the process model and worked through it with the participants focussing on provision and its relationship to each stage. The providers, who attended, found the model to be very helpful as a framework to support them to focus on areas they identified as most problematic and difficult, such as identifying and gathering evidence and demonstrating the impact of their provision, particularly on the end users. An important outcome of the trial was that working through the model with the providers and explaining it stage by stage was, in itself, regarded as an awareness raising process, which generated discussion and debate around a wide range of issues.

Having carried out this trial, we believe that model has genuine potential for use with providers (see Figure 8). Starting with the importance of a culture of professional learning and the need to contribute to its development by engaging with a continuous process of reflective practice, raises issues for providers about what is meant by reflective practice and what their role should be in developing a reflective learning culture themselves and through and within their provision. This places emphasis on what strategies providers can and should employ to ensure that their provision is underpinned by a model of reflective practice which supports education professionals to engage in a continuous self reflective process. It alerts providers to the need to encourage and support participants of their provision to engage in critical self assessment to identify their own learning needs, those of their pupils/students and of their organisations as the starting point for learning and development. This approach also places emphasis on the need for provision, which is linked directly to practice and which is sufficiently flexible in its form and delivery to allow for individual learning needs to be identified, addressed and supported. Moving on through the process model to the learning needs of the pupils/students and their assessment and identification raises issues for providers about the way in which they identify the learning outcomes of their provision and link these directly to impact on the end users. If the participants are going to select, or have selected, the provision with a view to meeting specific learning needs they have identified for themselves in relation to their pupils'/students' learning needs, a range of demands are placed on the provision, and indeed on the providers, in terms of modes of delivery, assessment procedures and evaluation.

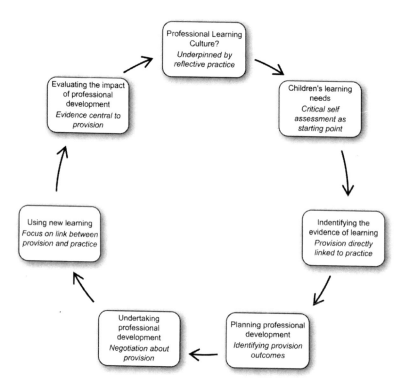

Figure 8. Using the model with providers.

These demands require providers to consider and allow for participants to negotiate, discuss and participate in the identification of learning outcomes of the provision. Throughout this stage of working through the model, there is also a concentration on evidence of impact, which is of considerable importance to providers because it requires that evidence of the direct link between the professional learning for the participants and that of the end-users is explicitly addressed as a feature of the provision. Using the model emphasises for the provider the need for a focus on evidence, the sort of evidence and its collection, to be central and integral to all aspects of the delivery, content, assessment and evaluation of the provision and has implications in particular for the adoption of an enquiry/research oriented approach to provision. Education professionals using the model will clearly identify and select provision which supports and enables them, not only to meet their identified learning needs, but also support and assist them to identify what evidence they will require to demonstrate that their own learning has impacted on that of their pupils/students and which focuses around the collection of that evidence.

Implementing learning and evaluating the impact of the professional learning as emphasised by the process model in the next stage are vitally important areas of consideration for providers and also have further implications for the mode of delivery of provision and the processes through which they evaluate their provision together with the participants. One off activities, with no follow up, which are not linked back to practice, will not enable participants, or indeed providers, to meet the demands of identifying the impact of professional learning on end users. Similarly evaluation through an end of session tick sheet or pro forma will not provide sufficient information about the value or impact of the provision in relation to practice and will certainly not provide information which will demonstrate evidence of impact on end users. Using the process model raises awareness for providers about the need to embed the professional learning in practice and to ensure that participants are supported to implement their new learning and to critically evaluate its impact on their own practice and to relate that impact through evidence to the identified learning needs of the pupils/students.

Challenges for Providers

Timperley et al., (2007) identify a professional learning process, which is in many ways similar to and certainly supports the process model. In summary it is a process through which the education professional engages in three cycles of enquiry; *What are our students' learning needs? What are our own learning needs? What has been the impact of our changed actions?* (p. xiiv). They point out that in order to address these enquiries effectively education professionals require complex and sophisticated assessment knowledge and tools. They also need to see themselves as agents of change and development and to be able to collect and analyse data systematically and effectively. They may require external expertise and support in order to do carry out these enquiries adequately and to meet the challenges of this critical self-assessment, self regulatory approach to monitoring and evaluating the impact of their professional learning on pupil/student outcomes. This also raises issues for providers of professional development opportunities and for their approach to provision. Challenging practice oriented learning activities which place emphasis on change and taking on the role of a change agent are demanded. A research oriented approach is also required but this must be supported by the requisite expertise and should be geared towards developing the essential sophisticated inquiry skills required to collect, analyse and evaluate evidence data effectively. These are far reaching implications for providers and for provision and raise serious questions about the quality of providers and their provision, which are discussed in Chapters 4, 5 and 6. In Chapter 4 we identified a number of essential factors which, we believe, can be seen as indicators of high quality professional development, against which providers might usefully measure their provision to evaluate whether it does in fact meet the challenges raised above so that provision

- engages participants actively in identification of their own professional development needs and supports them in that process;
- focuses on the learning needs of the end users and supports participants to identify and address;
- aims at change and transformation of professional practice as an outcome;
- develops knowledge and understanding at the participants own level;
- introduces, and supports the implementation of, new strategies and critical evaluation of their success;
- employs a research and enquiry approach which supports the identification, collection and evaluation of evidence of impact of participants professional learning;
- supports the development of a collaborative community of practice.

The process model is informed and underpinned by, and indeed depends upon, this view of professional development and provision. For providers these indicators, which are, by no means exhaustive, provide guidance for the development of provision, which has the potential to meet the learning needs of education professionals who are concerned to link their own learning directly to that of their pupils/students and to provide evidence of the impact of this process. We believe they provide a useful framework and guide for the development of provision, modes of delivery and at the same time provide support for assuring the quality of that provision. Using the process model, together with these indicators, providers can ensure that their provision is relevant to the learning needs not only of the participants of their provision but also for the end users. They will also be supported to meet, perhaps the even greater challenge of demonstrating the impact of their provision on both groups.

CHAPTER SUMMARY

It is important to recognise that issues relating to impact and evidence are of considerable concern to providers and as mentioned above this concern was voiced throughout the research we carried out for the PDB-PE (Keay and Lloyd, 2008) and in the trial described above. What also became apparent was that the majority of providers were anxious to develop strategies to address these vitally important areas and the PDB-PE based process of application for recognition was one which they welcomed because of the emphasis it places on both issues. They welcomed the opportunity to discuss evidence with us and were extremely enthusiastic about developing opportunities to share and disseminate good practice in the area. In order to facilitate this the PDB-PE has posted examples of successful applications on its website and holds workshops to support applicants and to enable them to interact and network with each other. What is apparent is that in addition to regarding impact and evidence as continuing problematic areas, providers are developing strategies to address them as demonstrated by the analysis of applications discussed above. However, this analysis also highlights a continuing lack of clarity over what constitutes evidence and in some cases a failure to address the issue at all.

Applying the process model to the development, implementation and evaluation of their provision has the potential to raise awareness about these issues further and to provide the necessary focus for providers on developing strategies, which will enable them to provide evidence of impact, in their evaluation of their provision, on the end users (see Figure 8). This was clearly demonstrated in the workshop trial referred to above. It also has the potential to support the participants of the provision to develop strategies for demonstrating the impact of their professional learning on their pupils/students. While there is no doubt that applying the model may initially raise many more questions and challenges than it provides answers and solutions, it can be seen to provide an extremely useful framework for thinking about provision, its design and purpose and for linking, and demonstrating that they are linking, outcomes with aims. We believe, therefore, that for the process model to be used effectively by education professionals and their institutions it should also be used at the same time by professional development providers to guide and inform decisions about the design, development, implementation and evaluation of their provision. This will ensure that education professionals are able to access provision which is appropriate and relevant to support their learning needs and will, at the same time, enable providers to demonstrate more effectively the value of their provision to practice and its impact on developing and enhancing pupils'/students' and their participants' learning and on the development of a high quality learning culture.

CHAPTER 11

CONCLUSION

This chapter provides a summary of the key issues and themes addressed in this book in relation to the developmental process model. It begins by looking briefly at the development of the model and assesses what has been achieved. Major findings arising from the pilot studies, which were carried out with a range of practitioners, to test it in use are used in this assessment. In Chapter 1 major themes, which informed the research leading to the development of the model and which underpin its effective use in practice, are identified as; *professional development, inclusive practice, reflective practice and enquiry* and *evidence and impact*. This chapter draws together the central issues explored and critically discussed in Chapters 1 – 10 in relation to those themes and to the model and its application in practice. Areas that require further professional engagement and research are identified and challenges are issued to readers to consider practical engagement in professional development planning using the impact driven process embodied in the model, which links their own learning directly to that of their pupils/students and places central importance on providing evidence to demonstrate the impact of their learning. The chapter concludes with some practical and organisational implications we identify for the future use of the model in practice.

THE DEVELOPMENT OF THE MODEL AND WHAT HAS BEEN ACHIEVED

As mentioned in Chapter 1, and throughout the book, the impetus to develop the model came from research with professional development providers (Keay & Lloyd, 2008a), who identified major concerns about how to demonstrate the impact of their provision on the end users, the pupils/students of the participants, of their provision. The central purpose of the research was to trial a process of self regulated quality assurance with the providers, as described in Chapter 6 in more detail, and through this research it became apparent that while they were very aware of the importance of providing evidence of impact as an indicator of high quality, they were confused and concerned about how to demonstrate that they were addressing it in and through their provision. It became clear from the evaluation of these findings together with the outcomes of our previous research in the areas of professional development, inclusive education and learning and teaching (see Appendix), that it would be useful to develop a tool or instrument which had the potential to support and enable a process of professional development planning, which centred around impact and evidence and which could be used by a wide range of education professionals in addition to providers. While we felt that it was important that this process should be impact/evidence driven we were also concerned that it should be a pupil/student centred, developmental process and not a reductionist tool which could be used to support a crude accountability procedure linking simplistic performance outcomes with professional development. This led to the development of a process model, rather than a tool or instrument, which we believe takes account of the complexity and problematic nature of assessing and identifying pupils'/students' needs and education professionals' learning needs and the relationship between them. It also recognises the vitally important role of the context in which the process takes place and we initially believed that an appropriate culture, as discussed in detail in Chapter 7, was a prerequisite. However, as a result of the research we now believe that using the model can also contribute to the development of an inclusive, supportive, enabling culture within the institution where it is used.

Just as the impetus for developing the model arose from interactive research with practising education professionals it was important for us to test it in use and to obtain feedback from a range of practitioners, a process which is documented and discussed in detail in Chapters 7-10. The outcomes of this piloting process have led us to a view that the model is, as we hoped it would be, useful on a number of levels and to a wide range of professionals. This process has also enabled us to refine and further develop the model, as discussed in Chapter 7, and to recognise its limitations. It was never the intention that the model should cover all aspects of professional learning and development, which as discussed in Chapter 2, may include a wide range and variety. For example, the identification and accessing of career and role oriented professional development may require a very different approach. The model is intended to focus on the impact of professional learning and development on children's learning by making a direct and overt link between the learners' identified needs and the learning required by the professional to address those needs. It is, therefore driven by the specific learning needs of the pupils/students and the learning of the professional is identified only in relation to the learning of the pupils/students as is the evidence to demonstrate its impact. In this sense it is a pupil/student centred model. What is clear, from the pilot studies we have carried out, is that engaging with the model and focusing in this way generates an awareness raising process for education professionals which informs their learning and development choices. It has implications for the form, content and delivery of that learning and at the same time supports the development of a culture where impact and evidence of impact are an integral part of assessing, monitoring and evaluating pupils'/students' learning. This awareness raising potential was a finding in the pilot studies, as discussed in Chapter 8 and 9 and also in the workshop trial with professional development providers discussed in Chapter 10.

It was clear from the pilot studies with practitioners that the process can be, and indeed should be, embedded in everyday professional practice. The characteristics of everyday practice developed through this process include a positive approach to learning, for professionals and children; an inclusive approach to teaching and learning; and a reflective and reflexive approach to all aspects of professional practice. The process challenges education professionals to identify their learning needs directly in relation to pupils' needs and to think of teaching and learning in relation to individuals rather than classes. In order to do this the process requires them to adopt a critically reflective approach to teaching and as a consequence to make, what may be in some circumstances, big changes to how they approach their work with pupils/students. The process also challenges professionals to ensure that they have a clear rationale for the selection of all professional development and to ensure that they match their specific learning needs and intended outcomes with professional learning activities. In relation to this they are challenged to link their learning with children's learning, to plan for the intended impact and ultimately to measure that impact.

As stated previously, it was always our intention that this model, and the process embedded in it, should be flexible enough to meet the needs of a wide range of education professionals. The stages outlined in the model (see Figure 5, Chapter 7) provide the essential elements but as discussed in relation to professional development providers (see Figure 8, Chapter 10) and leaders/managers they can be adapted to support professionals working in different roles and circumstances. The main challenge encountered in the school based pilot studies related to secondary school organisation and development conflict, particularly in relation to career related development and undertaking accredited programmes. Secondary schools are usually organised in subject areas, the staff are based in subject groups and the pupils/students are taught subjects and for some of the more marginal subjects where time was limited to one session per week, this challenged the use of the process model, as discussed in detail in Chapter 8. In this case a possible solution is to focus on the identification of generic learning needs for both the pupils and the education professionals. The model has the potential to raise professional confidence through analysing professional effectiveness. It also has the potential to give professionals control of their own development and to ensure that they take responsibility for effective professional development. The potential of the process model for practitioners is dependent on their leaders/managers and the organisational and cultural context they develop and promote. Naturally, there are numerous challenges and opportunities for leaders and managers in considering and using the process model.

Using the process model and its stages challenges leaders to consider the nature of the role they are undertaking; for example, is it a leadership role or merely a management role? Related to this question are cultural considerations such as the need for a collective vision for the organisation and how this is achieved, although this may initially have to be developed through small groups such as subject teams. The cultural prerequisites for the model to work may not be in place initially and therefore a leader will be challenged to demonstrate commitment to achieving such a professional culture. Other more managerial challenges can also be seen as opportunities, for example, managing staff performance through the model without imposing managerial professionalism and managing resources and staff impression of resource allocation. Using the model has clear benefits for leaders/managers of an individual and organisational nature. It can support the development of a professional learning community, it can be used to guide staff and to help all concerned to take the provision of professional development seriously. It has the potential to help to achieve consistent management practices in relation to professional development and to help consideration of value for money and time. In addition, it can, as discussed in Chapter 9, support leaders and managers in their own professional development.

In the workshop trial, which we carried out with twenty two providers, it was clear that using the process model in a process of evaluating their provision was useful and enhancing. They reported that it made them aware that their provision should include opportunities for participants to focus on the identification of their pupils'/students' learning needs as well as their own and that it should provide a more flexible range of activities to support this process. This also had implications for more flexible approaches to delivery and content, which would enable participants to bring their own agendas to the learning activities in the provision. As in the initial research with providers, which inspired the development of the model, issues surrounding evidence and what counts as evidence of impact were raised and debated vigorously. However the process demanded by the model which, as part of the identification of pupils'/students' needs also requires the identification of what evidence will be required in order to demonstrate that those needs have been addressed, was seen by the providers as particularly important and supportive. They felt that if participants have engaged with this process as a means to identify their own learning and development needs, before they attend the provision, they will inevitably be more focused on issues surrounding impact and the evidence required to demonstrate that impact. For providers then the issue is how to make their provision supportive to the process and to address through it the individual needs of the participants. One of the strategies suggested by the providers in the workshop trial was to employ a more participative enquiry based approach to learning and development activities and all agreed on the need to include more opportunities for participants to engage with collecting, analysing and evaluating practice based data. These approaches are also identified by Timperley et al., (2007) as key to professional development provision, which will support and enable education professionals to address the learning needs of their pupils more effectively. They go further and suggest the need to incorporate sophisticated strategies for assessing and identifying learning needs such as training in interrogating, analysing and evaluating data and teaching research and enquiry techniques.

The model was developed to support a wide range of education professionals and what is clear from the feedback obtained from this workshop trial with twenty two providers is that it is certainly useful and has the potential to support the development of more effective provision, which is relevant not only to the learning needs of the participants but also to those of the end users. Using the model involves a shift in thinking and approach for providers to focus on the learning needs of end users of provision as the starting point for the development of provision and also for its content, modes of delivery and evaluation. The process provides questions that providers should expect participants to have considered before electing to engage with the provision and also while they engage in the learning process. It does therefore have the potential to be used by providers and participants to ensure that a coherent approach is achieved. As discussed below there is further potential here for research and for development of the model but we believe that, in its current form, it can contribute to the development of high quality professional development provision which addresses and has the potential to meet the indicators identified in Chapter 4, when providers work through the design and evaluation of their provision.

As mentioned in the introduction to this chapter, throughout the book we have identified major themes, which we regard as crucial to the underpinning, development and implementation of the model in practice and the following sections highlight our concluding thoughts about those themes in relation to the model.

Professional Development

Chapter 2 introduces professional development and examines it through explorations of its definition, how it is undertaken, how it is supported, led and managed. It also draws on different versions of professionalism to understand how they will affect cultures, organisation, approaches to leadership and ultimately professional development. In subsequent chapters we use these discussions to interrogate the relationship between professional learning and children's learning. Throughout the book we have returned to, developed and applied the sub-themes of responsibility, control, professional knowledge, professional learning communities and personalising professional development in order to make suggestions for the improvement of professional development.

At a practical level, developing and piloting the process model has shown that it has the potential to expand understanding of professional development through consideration of different knowledge types. Participants started to expand their understanding of the uses of different forms of professional development and this led to them carefully considering what form of development activity they undertook. Their choices became less random and more relevant to their learning needs in relation to the children's learning needs. This developing understanding had an impact on the roles of leaders and managers in how they supported professional development and what forms of professional development were provided and resourced. Linked to leadership and management, issues concerning responsibility and control were raised in relation to professional development and forms of professionalism are considered throughout the book.

The culture of an organisation is influenced by the form of professionalism adopted by those in leadership roles and the nature of this influence is a theme running through the book. The pilot studies supported our belief that a democratic form of professionalism will not only enable the model to be used, but also the intended outcomes to be achieved. As outlined in Table 1, the characteristics of democratic professionalism when related to professional development, relate very clearly to the model's intentions. Professional development is

– Self regulated
– Initiated by the individual
– Collaborative and collegial

- Reviewed by the individual through critically reflective practice
- Driven by pupil needs
- Focused on an inclusive approach to education which builds knowledge and is enquiry driven

Where these characteristics were not in place, as was the case in one of the pilot studies, the nature of professional learning becomes externally controlled with compliance as the driving force, meaning that change is slow in taking place. Any development that does take place is not assessed by the individual but externally reviewed, driven by efficiency objectives and motivated by self interest.

Inclusive Practice

There are two major issues concerning inclusive practice, which can be identified as themes running throughout this book and which have impacted on the development of the model and its implementation in practice. The first is the policy for inclusion and the requirement for education professionals to develop more inclusive approaches to practice and the second, which is connected but different, is that the model requires an inclusive context and culture in the institution in order to be used effectively. In both cases, we believe, the model has potential.

Turning to the first issue, in Chapter 3 we discuss, albeit briefly, the implications of the move in recent years towards more inclusion and the pressure to develop more inclusive approaches to practice, which can be identified as policy initiatives not only in England but internationally (Pijl, Meijer & Hegarty, 1997; Dyson, 1999; Barton & Armstrong, 2007; Armstrong, Armstrong & Spandagou, 2010). This has clearly put pressure on education professionals and had major implications for their professional development and learning. It has also resulted in the development of a range of new roles; new responsibilities; new modes of working; a much wider range of ability in the pupil/student population of mainstream schools; changes in the roles of special schools, units and support services and considerable pressure on the whole range of education professionals to change and develop approaches to practice. Clearly these changes and developments have impacted, and continue to impact, considerably on the professional learning and development choices and needs of education professionals and also, more importantly, we believe, on the learning needs of the pupils/students they work with. Using the process model is, we believe, a useful support to education professionals facing these considerable challenges and seeking to change and develop their practice. The model requires professionals to engage with a developmental process which is learning focused and which is premised on the notion that in order to meet the learning needs of the pupils/students professionals will need to identify and access new learning themselves. It assumes change and development as integral parts of the process and assists and supports them in a very structured process to evaluate that change and development, with the provision of continuous feedback, in the form of evidence of impact, as a key feature of the process. The model enables users, therefore, to cope with the processes of change and development realistically and strategically.

Throughout the book we have also placed emphasis on the importance of using the model within, and as part of the development of, a professional learning community and this is another way in which it can support professionals faced with the pressures of developing more inclusive approaches to practice. Inclusion and inclusive practice require the development of more multi professional collaborative practice if the learning needs of all pupils are to be addressed effectively, as discussed in Chapters 3 and 6. During the pilot studies referred to above and discussed fully in Chapters 7-10, participants often turned to colleagues and/or coaches within the institution, to supply them with, or support them to access, the professional learning they identified as necessary. Collaborative teaching and peer observation were also cited as important professional learning activities. Using the process model, together with line managers, within a supportive institution seemed to encourage and develop this sort of collaborative approach to professional learning and development, which in turn has the potential to contribute to the development of more inclusive approaches to practice.

The second major issue, identified above, concerning inclusive practice, is the inclusive context and culture in which the model is used. During the development of the model the importance of the culture of the institution in which the model is used became increasingly clear. A supportive learning environment, which places emphasis on professional learning and adopts an approach to the identification of the learning needs of professionals, which is developmental, individual and personalised, as discussed in detail in Chapters 2 and 7, is essential. Similarly an approach to the identification and assessment of pupil'/students' learning needs, which involves the pupils/students themselves, is holistic and builds positively on what they *can* do rather than focusing on what they *can't* do, is equally essential, as discussed fully in Chapter 6. These approaches can also be seen as inclusive approaches to learning and teaching as key to the development of more inclusive practice (Lloyd, 2000; 2008). In the pilot studies it was clear that where this sort of institutional approach was taken in relation to learning, teaching, assessment, professional learning and development, the model worked most effectively. Indeed, we believe that this sort of institutional approach, or at least the intention to develop this sort of approach, is a pre-requisite for the model to be used effectively and it is incorporated into the processes of the model in Stage 1. What has become clear, however, through the pilot studies, is the potential of the model to raise awareness about the importance of this sort of inclusive approach to practice and to contribute to its development within an institution. Thus using the process model, which focuses on what can be seen as inclusive approaches to practice and depends upon an inclusive supportive learning culture, is in itself a developmental process for the institution, which can contribute to the development that culture.

CHAPTER 11

Reflective Practice and Enquiry

The development of reflective practice and enquiry in education, and in particular in the learning and development of education professionals, has long been identified as crucially important (Friere 1973; Carr & Kemmis 1986; Schon 1987; Kemmis 2005; Timperley et al., 2007). An approach to practice, which is critically reflective and employs enquiry as a method to address change and development is essential to the effective use of the model. The model requires an enquiry approach to identifying the learning strengths and needs of the pupils and then makes demands on the education professional to critically reflect on her/his own practice to identify her/his learning needs. The identification, collection, interrogation and evaluation of evidence to demonstrate impact, as an integral part of this process, also require the adoption of an enquiry approach. Working through the stages of the process, as described in Chapter 7, requires, and indeed assists the education professional to develop, a self critical and reflective approach. Through the stages of the process the user is challenged, assisted by the questions and prompts provided, to critically reflect on all aspects of her/his effectiveness in role; in assessing and identifying learning needs and outcomes; in learning and teaching; as a learner her/himself; in developing and changing her/his practice; and in collecting and demonstrating evidence of all these. The intention is that this process model will become an integral part of the daily practice of education professionals as they use it and that the reflection and enquiry processes necessary to use it will be enhanced, developed and incorporated into their practice. It became clear during the pilot studies, however, that participants did not always have the skills necessary to reflect on aspects of their effectiveness. There was a tendency to focus on weaknesses rather than strengths and to be overwhelmed by what they perceived as their learning needs. Similarly when reflecting on the pupils'/students' learning needs they were often unable to focus down on specific learning needs and there was a tendency to identify large scale projects for change or development. Problems were also clear in relation to taking an enquiry approach to identifying, analysing and evaluating evidence and relating it to learning outcomes and impact and support was required to work through the reflective process with some participants. If reflective practice and enquiry are, then, essential to the model's effective use it is important that opportunities are provided to learn about how to develop and use them. While it is clear that working through the process required to use the model supports the development of these skills, there would seem to be a place for further research and perhaps further development of the model in this area, which is discussed further below.

Impact and Evidence

While it requires a developmental, pupil/student, learning centred process, the model is driven by the need to demonstrate the impact of professional learning on pupils'/students' learning through evidence. Problematic issues surrounding what counts as evidence of impact and how to collect and use it were, as mentioned above, a driving force in its development and are therefore centrally important to its effective use. Pilot studies and the workshop trial identified that while the focus and emphasis on impact and evidence were welcomed by participants there remain issues about, what counts as evidence, what sorts of evidence should be collected and how to use it. Participants in the pilot studies required support and guidance to identify suitable evidence and often fell back on tests as the easiest form of evidence of impact even though it was difficult to demonstrate the impact relationship between their professional learning and the learning of the pupil/students through these. Thus while the model raises awareness of the need to demonstrate impact and enables and supports users to focus on how, what and when evidence might be collected there is still work to be done. We believe that incorporating the model into daily practice so that it becomes an integral part of that practice is important here, so that focusing on impact and evidence become a normal part of learning needs identification and assessment and professional learning and development planning. It is also important, as discussed in Chapters 6 and 8, to involve the pupils/students in the processes of identifying and assessing their learning needs, planning learning targets and deciding what evidence will demonstrate that learning has taken place. Involving pupils in the identification and collection of evidence, in this way, ties decisions about it directly to the identified learning needs and outcomes and can broaden the range and variety of evidence. It also ensures that evidence collected is appropriate, more relevant and provides more useful feedback about the learning which has taken place which can be used, as discussed in Chapter 6 and shown in figure 1, to identify future learning needs.

POTENTIAL FOR FURTHER RESEARCH

As identified in the earlier sections of this chapter, while the model has proved to be useful and developmental in the pilot studies and the workshop trial with providers there are areas for further research and development. It is not set in tablets of stone as it is a process model, founded on developmental principles and it was always the intention that users would modify and adapt it to make it more appropriate for their own needs. We hope, and indeed intend, that further use of the model by education professionals and feedback from them, as they use and develop it as part of their practice, will inform the identification of further research in this important area of education. It is clear that much work remains to be done in relation to evidence, what counts as evidence, how and when to collect it and how to use it effectively to examine the link between professional learning and pupils'/students' learning and to demonstrate impact. The development of inclusive, holistic approaches to identifying and assessing pupils'/students' learning needs also requires more research and we believe that using the model, with professionals and pupils/students, as part of a collaborative, participative research process, could be an important strategy to investigate this area. It is also important to return to the group of professionals from whom the impetus to design the model came and to investigate how it might be further developed and/or modified to assist them in the development of high quality provision which links directly to the learning of end users as well as participants and enables them to demonstrate its impact on both groups.

In conclusion, we believe the next steps with regard to the model are to encourage a wide range of education professionals, in a variety of schools/institutions, to engage with it as an integral part of their daily practice. For this to be successful it will be necessary to adopt the model as part of a whole school/institution approach to learning and professional learning and development. The culture of school/institution will need to be inclusive, or at the very least to be striving towards such an approach. It will need to be supportive and encourage the development of a professional learning community, of the sort referred to throughout the book. It will also need to engage with a democratic approach to professionalism, as discussed in Chapter 2 and above. We believe that if these requirements are met, using the model will prove to be a useful and supportive strategy, which will enhance practice, and contribute to the further development of the culture.

APPENDIX

DEVELOPING THE MODEL

Our previous research has contributed to the development of the ideas, which have informed and underpin the model presented in this book. The projects have taken place over a 25 year period and a summary of each one is presented below.

Defining and Understanding Inclusion and Inclusive Practice (C. Lloyd)

Theoretical research and analysis of the concepts of inclusion and inclusive practice and critical analysis of national and international education policies in which they are promoted.

This research was developed initially through an MA Curriculum Studies and further through a PhD. Post doctoral research led to publications in the form of book chapters and peer-reviewed articles. Professional development courses at masters and doctoral level developed and taught around this research nationally and internationally since 1986. Outcomes of this research process have influenced the development of the model in two major ways. Firstly by making clear the increased pressure on education professionals to develop more inclusive approaches to practice and to access professional learning and development to support them with this. Secondly in our conviction that the model requires, but also has the potential to develop, an inclusive culture and context to be used effectively.

Classroom Management – Managing Collaborative Learning and Teaching (C. Lloyd)

Longitudinal action research project carried out collaboratively with a colleague, (Jeff Beard), in special and mainstream schools from 1986 to 1991.

This research led to a number publications, including a book, and also to considerable professional development work with teachers throughout a large London borough and in the University of Greenwich CPD programme (1991-1998). Areas of investigation included;

– Collaborative teaching
– Managing small group work
– Learning through investigative approaches
– Managing classroom behaviour
– Supporting the development of active learning
– Independent learning
– Flexible approaches to assessment
– Pupil self assessment

The influence of this research is clear in the model presented in this book, which relies upon flexible, collaborative assessment of learning and teaching, which involves and recognises the importance of pupils/students. The importance of developing a collaborative professional learning community as part of the learning culture of institutions, clearly reflected in this research can also be found in the underpinning of the model.

Developing and Changing Practice Through Critically Reflective Action Research (C.Lloyd)

> Case study carried out with a cohort of students on a postgraduate programme offered to practising education professionals working in the Netherlands, between 2002 and 2005.

The three-year programme of study was a practice-based programme of professional development, with heavy emphasis on action research throughout. For this particular group action research was an entirely new concept, and indeed many of them expressed considerable scepticism about its validity as an approach to research, or for that matter, professional development, at the beginning of the programme. The whole group was working in areas associated with SEN where the need to change practice was an urgent imperative, due to changes in education policy and the rapid move towards inclusion. Findings indicated the importance of an active critically reflective approach to research and enquiry for practising professionals who want to develop, change and improve their practice.

Teachers' Professional Development in the Induction Phase (J.Keay)

> A series of research projects carried out with newly qualified teachers during their first years in the teaching profession (2000 – 2008).

Research was carried out in part fulfilment of a PhD with newly qualified teachers of physical education, exploring how their professional development impacted on their teaching practice. This was further developed in two successive projects with teachers in their first 3 years of the profession. The findings, which have been published in peer-reviewed journals, suggest that school based professional development and in particular close colleagues, are highly influential in new teachers' development.

Essentially Dance Evaluation Project (J.Keay)

> An evaluation of a pilot project to provide professional development for teachers and teaching assistants to enable them to introduce ballroom and Latin American dance into their schools (undertaken with Jon Spence).

The participants in this project were expected to cascade the professional development to colleagues on their schools and introduce the dance to pupils. The dance projects were highly successful but data gathered from the participants suggested that the cascade model was problematic and that the professional development needed to be more specific to participants' needs.

Continuing Professional Development for Talent Development in Physical Education, Monitoring and Evaluation Report (J.Keay & C.Lloyd)

Evaluation of two phases of a cascade model of professional development provided for teachers by the Youth Sport Trust, between 2006 and 2008.

The overall aim of the project was to monitor and evaluate the impact of professional development programmes with Local Delivery Agents and the school sports partnership networks, the latter being the intended recipients of the cascading of gifted and talented PE information. We found evidence of impact on the practice of the disseminators but only limited evidence of impact on pupil learning and achievement during the two years of the programme. Much evidence cited about the impact on pupils was based on the perceptions of workshop attendees rather than on tangible evidence. The evidence supported the view that they needed help in developing a more detailed systematic process for the collection of evidence and analysis of the impact of their professional development provision.

PDB –PE Research – Measuring the Impact of Quality Standards on Professional Development (J.Keay & C.Lloyd)

Longitudinal research carried out to evaluate a set of quality standards against which professional development providers working in the areas of Physical Education and sport, can measure their provision.

The research, which began in 2005, adopted an Action Research approach. It was carried out in three stages: *Stage 1*: Exploration of practice with providers to ensure the appropriateness of the quality standards. *Stage 2*: Following implementation of the standards, an investigation to find out if and how they are used. *Stage 3*: Gathering in depth information from a small number of providers that are using the standards, to identify and measure impact for the dissemination of findings to the profession and to identify case study material demonstrating good practice. During the research process providers raised issues of concern about how they should demonstrate the impact of their provision on the end users, pupils/students of the participants. They were also concerned about how and what to identify in terms of evidence. These findings contributed significantly to and provided the impetus for the development of the model presented in this book.

REFERENCES

Ainscow (2003) Using teacher development to foster inclusive classrooms in T. Booth, K. Nes, & M. Stromstad, (Eds) (2003) *Developing Inclusive Teacher Education* London: Routledge Falmer.

Alderman, G. & Brown, R. (2005) Can Quality Assurance Survive the Market? Accreditation and audit at the Crossroads, *Higher Education*, 59 (4), 313–328.

Alexandrou, A., Field, K. & Mitchell, H. (2005) *The Continuing Professional Development of Educators: emerging European issues*, Oxford: Symposium.

Anderson, S. (2002) *Working Together to Develop a Professional Working Community* in Report of Higher Education Research Development Society of Australia Annual Conference pp. 20–26, Perth Western Australia.

Apple, M. (2009) Foreword, in S. Gewirtz, P. Mahony, I. Hextall, & A. Cribb (Eds.) *Changing Teacher Professionalism: International trends, challenges and ways forward*, London: Routledge.

Armour, K. (2006) Physical education teachers as career-long learners: a compelling research agenda *Physical Education and Sport Pedagogy*, 11 (3), 203–207.

Armour, K. (2010) The physical education profession and its professional responsibility ... or ... why '12 weeks paid holiday' will never be enough, *Physical Education and Sport Pedagogy*, 15 (1), 1–13.

Armstrong, A.C., Armstrong, D. & Spandagou, I. (2010) *Inclusive Education, International Policy & Practice*. London: Sage.

Armstrong, F., Armstrong, D. & Barton, L. (Eds.) (2000) *Inclusive education*, London: David Fulton.

Bagley, (2007) Dalit Children in India: challenges for education and inclusiveness in Verma, G.K, Bagley, C. R. & Mohan, J.H.A. (2007) *International Perspectives on Educational diversity and Inclusion*, London: Routledge.

Ball, S. (1990) *Markets, Morality and Equality in Education* London: Tufnell.

Ball, S. J. (2008) *The Education Debate*, Bristol: Policy Press.

Barber, B. (2008), *Consumed: how markets corrupt children, infantilise adults, and swallow citizens whole*. London: W.W. Norton.

Barber, M. & Mourshed, M. (2007) *How the world's best performing school systems come out on top*, McKinsey, http://www.mckinsey.com/App-Media/reports/SSO/Worlds_School_Systemss_Final.pdf.

Barton, L & Armstrong, F. (2007) *Policy, Experience and Change: Cross Cultural Reflections on Inclusive Education* London. Springer

Barton, L. (1995) Segregated Special Education, some critical observations, in G. Zarb, (ed) *Researching Disabling Barriers*, London: London Policy Studies Institute.

Baumfield, V. (2006) Tools for Pedagogical Inquiry: The impact of teaching thinking skills on teachers, *Oxford Review of Education*, 32 (2), 185–196.

Baumfield, V. & Butterworth, M. (2005) Developing and Sustaining Professional Dialogue about Teaching and Learning in Schools, *Journal of In-Service Education*, 31 (2), 297–331.

Beach, D. & Dovemark, M. (2009) Making 'right' choices? An ethnographic account of creativity, performativity and personalised learning policy, concepts and practices, *Oxford Review of Education*, 35 (6), 689–704.

Beck, J. (2008) 'Governmental Professionalism: Re-professionalising or Deprofessionalising Teachers in England', British Journal of Educational Studies, 56 (2) pp. 119–143.

Beck, J. (2009) Appropriating professionalism: restructuring the official knowledge base of England's 'modernised' teaching profession, *British Journal of Sociology of Education*, 30 (1), 3–14.

Beckett, D. and Hagar, P. (2002) *Life, work and learning: Practice in postmodernity*, London: Routledge.

Benjamin, S. (2002) *The micropolitics of inclusive education*. Buckingham: Open University Press.

Billett, S. (2001) Learning through working life: interdependencies at work, *Studies in Continuing Education*, 23 (1), 19–35.

REFERENCES

Blackmore, A. (2004). A critical evaluation of academic internal review, *Quality Assurance in Education*, 12 (3), 128–135.

Bolam, R. (1999) The Emerging Conceptualisation of INSET: does this constitute professional development?, Standing *Committee for the Education and Training of Teachers: Teacher Professionalism and the State in the 21st Century*, Annual Conference, Rugby, 26–28 November.

Bolam, R. (2000) Emerging Policy Trends: some implications for continuing professional development, *Journal of In-service Education*, 26 (2), 267–280.

Bolam, R. & Weindling, D. (2006) *Synthesis of research and evaluation projects concerned with capacity building through teachers' professional development*, Report for General Teaching Council for England.

Bolam, R., McMahon, A., Stoll, L., Thomas, S. & Wallace, M. (2005) *Creating and sustaining effective professional learning communities* Research Report 635, Bristol, University of Bristol.

Booth, T., Nes, K. & Stromstad, M. (2003) *Developing Inclusive Teacher Education*, London: Routledge Falmer.

Borko, H. (2004) Professional Development and Teacher Learning: mapping the terrain, *Educational Researcher*, 42 (1), 3–15.

Bowe, J., Gore, J. & Elsworth, W. (2010) Rounding out professional development: Professional Learning Community, Instructional Rounds and Quality Teaching, paper presented at *Australian Association for research in Education, Annual Conference*, 28th November – 2nd December, 2010, Melbourne.

Brown, S., Edmonds, S., & Lee, B. (2002) *Continuing Professional Development: LEA and school support for teachers*, Slough: NFER.

Bruner, J. (1986) *Actual Minds Possible Worlds*, Cambridge, MA: Harvard University Press.

Bubb, S., Earley, P., & Hempel-Jorgensen, A., (2008) *Staff Development Outcomes Study Report*, for Training and Development Agency (TDA).

Burchell, H., Dyson, J. & Rees, M. (2002) Making a Difference: a study of the impact of Continuing Professional Development on professional practice, *Journal of In-Service Education*, 28 (2), 219–229.

Burns, C. (2005) Tensions between National School and Teacher Development Needs: as survey of teachers' views about continuing professional development within a group of schools, *Journal of In-Service Education*, 31 (2), 353–372.

Bush, T. (2003) *Theories of Educational Leadership and Management*, London: Sage.

Carr, W. & Kemmis, S. (1986) *Becoming Critical: Educational Knowledge and Action Research*, Lewes: Falmer Press.

Chapman, C. (2002) Ofsted and School improvement: teachers' perceptions of the inspection process in schools facing challenging circumstances. *School Leadership and Management*, 22 (3), 257–272.

Charmaz, K. (2006) *Constructing Grounded Theory: A practical guide through qualitative analysis*, London: Sage.

Children, Schools and Families Committee (2010) *Training of Teachers*, House of Commons London: The Stationery Office Limited.

Clement, M. & Vandenburghe, R. (2001) How School Leaders can Promote Teachers' Professional Development: an account from the field, *School Leadership and Management*, 21 (1), 43–57.

Corbett, J. & Slee, R. (2000), An international conversation on inclusive education in D. Armstrong, & L. Barton (Eds.) *Inclusive Education.Policy, Contexts andComparative Education*, London: David Fulton.

Cordingley, P. (1997) Making Research Work for You, *Professional Development Today*, October, 59–63.

Cordingley, P. (2008) Qualitative Study of School Level Strategies for Teachers' CPD, *Centre for the Use of Research and Evidence in Education*, Coventry, CUREE.

Cordingley, P., Bell, M., Evans, D., & Firth, A. (2005) The impact of collaborative CPD on classroom teaching and learning. Review: What do teacher impact data tell us about collaborative CPD?, *Research Evidence in Education Library*. London: EPPI-Centre, Social Science Research Unit, Institute of Education, University of London.

Cordingley, P., Bell, M., Rundell, B., Evans, D. & Curtis, A. (2003) The impact of collaborative CPD on classroom teaching and learning, *Research Evidence in Education Library.* London: EPPI-Centre, Social Science Research Unit, Institute of Education, University of London.

Centre for the Use of Research and Evidence in Education (CUREE) (2010) *Postgraduate Professional Development (PPD) Programme Quality Assurance Strand, Research Report Year 3*, Report for TDA, accessed 2.10.10, www.tda.gov.uk/teacher/developing-career/professional-development/ppd/benefits.aspx.

Crick, R. D. (2009), Pedagogical challenges for personalisation: integrating the personal and the public through context-driven enquiry, *The Curriculum Journal*, 20 (3),185–189.

Danaher, P., Gale, T. & Erben, T. (2000) The Teacher Educator as (Re) Negotiated Professional: critical incidents in steering between state and market in Australia, *Journal of Education for Teaching*, 26 (1), 55–71.

Day, C. (1999) *Developing Teachers: the challenges to lifelong learning*, London: Falmer Press.

Day, C. (2000) Teachers in the Twenty-First Century: time to renew the vision, *Teachers and Teaching: theory and practice*, 6 (1), 101–115.

Day, C. (2002) The Challenge to be the Best: reckless curiosity and mischievous motivation (1), *Teachers and Teaching: theory and practice*, 8, (3 / 4), 421–434.

Day, C. & Qing Gu (2010) *The New Lives of Teachers*, Abingdon: Routledge.

Darling-Hammond, L., Chung Wei, R., Andree, A., Richardson, N., & Orphanos, S. (2009) *Professional Learning in the Learning Profession: A status report on teacher development in the United States and abroad*, www.nsdc.org/news/NSDCstudy2009.pdf.

Desimone, L. (2009) Improving Impact Studies of Teachers' Professional Development: Towards better Conceptualizations and Measures, *Education Researcher*, 38, pp. 181–199 http://www.aera.net. Accessed 10.09.

DCSF (Department for Children, Schools and Families) (2008) *Being the best for our children: Releasing talent for teaching and learning*, Nottingham: DCSF.

DES (Department of Education and Science) (1977) *In-Service Training: The Role of Colleges and Departments* (Report on Education No. 88), London: HMSO.

DES (Department of Education and Science) (1978) *Special Educational Needs: Report of the Committee of Enquiry into the Education of Handicapped Children and Young People, The Warnock Report*, London. HMSO.

DfEE (Department for Education and Employment) (1997) *Excellence for All children: meeting special educational needs*, London: DfEE.

DfES (Department for Education and Skills) (2001) *Special Educational Needs: Code of Practice*, London: DfES.

DfES (Department for Education and Skills) (2001b) *Schools Achieving Success*, London: DfES.

DfES (Department for Education and Skills) (2004) *Removing Barriers to Achievement. The Government's Strategy for SEN*, London: DfES.

DfES (Department for Education and Skills) (2003) *National Teacher Research Panel: Engaging teacher expertise* Working document [online], DfES, available from http://www.dfes.gov.uk.

DfES (Department for Education and Skills) (2004) *Every Child Matters: Change for Children*, London: Her Majesty's Stationery Office.

DfES (Department for Education and Skills) (2006) *2020 vision: Report of the Teaching and Learning in 2020 Review Group*, Nottingham: DfES.

Dewey, J. (1963) *Experience and Education*, New York: Macmillan.

Doecke, B., Parr, G. & North, S. (2008) *National Mapping of Teacher Professional Learning*, Melbourne: Monash University.

Dunleavy, P. & Hood, C. (1994) From Old Public Administration to New Public Management, *Public Money and Management*, 14 (3), 9–16.

Dyson, A. (1999) Inclusion and Inclusions: theories and discourses in inclusive education in H. Daniels & P. Garner, *Inclusive Education*, London: Kogan Page.

Dyson, A. (2001) Special Educational Needs in the twenty first century: where we've been and where we're going, *British Journal of Special Educational Needs*, 28(1), 24–28.

REFERENCES

Elliott, J. (2007) Assessing the quality of action research, *Research Papers in Education*, 22(2), 229–246.

Eraut, M. (1994) *Developing Professional Knowledge and Competence*, London: Falmer Press.

Evetts, J. (2003) The sociological analysis of Professionalism: occupational change in the modern world, *International Sociology*, 18 (2), 395–415.

Evetts, J. (2009) The management of professionalism: a contemporary paradox, in S. Gewirtz, P. Mahony, I. Hextall, & A. Cribb, *Changing Teacher Professionalism: International trends, challenges and ways forward*, pp.19–30, London: Routledge.

Field, K. (2005) Continuing Professional Development for Leaders and Teachers: the English Perspective in A. Alexandrou, K. Field, & H. Mitchell (Eds.) *The Continuing Professional Development of Educators: emerging European issues*, Oxford: Symposium Books.

Friedman, A. & Phillips, M. (2004) Continuing professional development: developing a vision, *Journal of Education and Work*, 17 (3), 361–376.

Fielding, M. (2006) Leadership, personalisation and high performance schooling: Naming the new totalitarianism, *School Leadership and Management*, 26 (4), 347–369.

Forde, C., McMahon, M., McPhee, A. & Patrick, F. (2006) *Professional Development, reflection and enquiry*, London, Paul Chapman Publishing.

Friere, P. (1973), *Education for Critical Consciousness*, New York: Continuum.

Furlong, J., Barton, L., Miles, S., Whiting, C. & Whitty, G. (2000) *Teacher Education in Transition: re-forming professionalism*, Buckingham: Open University Press.

Garet, S., Porter, C., Desimone, L., Birman, B. & Suk Yoon, K. (2001) What Makes Professional Development Effective? Results from a national sample of teachers, *American Educational Research Journal*, 38 (4), 915–945.

General Teaching Council for England (2007) *A Personalised Approach to Continuing Professional Development (CPD) – Advice to the Secretary of State for education on effective, relevant and sustained CPD*, London: GTCE.

General Teaching Council for England (GTC) (2005) *What do studies of CPD tell us about the factors which help professional growth of teachers and pupil learning?* www.gtce.org.uk/research/romtopics/rom_cpd/cpd_dec05/, accessed 1.10.08.

Gilbert, C. (2006) *2020 vision: Report of the teaching and learning in 2020 Review Group*. Nottingham.

Gerwirtz, S. (2002) *The Managerial School: post welfarism and social justice in education*, London: Routledge.

Gewirtz, S., Mahony, P., Hextall, I. & Cribb, A. (2009) *Changing Teacher Professionalism: International trends, challenges and ways forward*, London: Routledge.

Giroux, H. (1990). Critical thinking and the politics of culture and voice: rethinking thediscourses of education, in R. Sherman & R. Webb (Eds.) *Qualitative Research inEducation: Focus and Methods*, London: Falmer Press.

Ingvarson, L; Meiers, M & Beavis, A. (2005) Factors Affecting Impact of Professional Development Programs on Teachers' Knowledge, Practice, Students Outcomes & Efficacy, *Education Policy Analysis Archives*, 13 (10), 1–20.

Glaser, B.G. & Strauss, A.L. (1967) *The Discovery of Grounded Theory: Strategies for qualitative research*, New York: Aldine de Gruyter.

Goldschmidt, P. & Phelps, G. (2010) Does teacher professional development affect content and pedagogical knowledge: How much and for how long?, *Economics of Education Review*, 29: 432–439.

Gorard, S. (2001) The Role of Cause and Effect in Education as a Social Science, *Economic and Social Research Council Teaching and Learning Research Programme, Research Capacity Building Network* [online], Paper 43, Cardiff University, available from http://www.cardiff.ac.uk/socsi/capacity, [accessed 9.1.04].

Guskey, T. (2000) *Evaluating Professional Development*, Thousand Oaks CA: Corwin Press.

Guskey, T. (2002) Professional Development and Teacher Change, *Teachers and Teaching: theory and practice*, 8 (3 / 4), 381–391.

Hammersley, M. (1992) *What's Wrong with Ethnography?* London: Routledge.

Hargreaves, A. (1994) *Changing Teachers Changing Times*, London: Cassell.

Layder, D. (1993) *New Strategies in Social Research*, Cambridge: Polity Press.

Hargreaves, A. & Goodson, I. (1996) Teachers' Professional Lives: aspirations and actualities, in I. Goodson and A. Hargreaves (Eds.) *Teachers' Professional Lives*, London: Falmer Press, 1–27.

Harland, J. & Kinder, K. (1997) Teachers' Continuing Professional Development: framing a model of outcomes, *British Journal of In-service Education*, 23 (1), 71–84.

Hartley, D. (2008) Education, Markets and The Pedagogy of Personalisation, *British Journal of Education Studies*. 56 (4), 423–434.

Hartley, D. (2009) Personalisation: the nostalgic revival of child-centred education?, *Journal of Education Policy*, 24(4): 423–434.

Hegarty, S. (2000) Teaching as a Knowledge-Based Activity, *Oxford Review of Education*, 26 (3/4), 451–465.

Helsby, G. (1995) Teachers' Construction of Professionalism in England in the 1990s, *Journal of Education for Teaching*, 21 (3), 317–332.

Helsby, G. (1999) *Changing Teachers' Work*, Buckingham: Open University Press.

Hiebert, J., Gallimore, R. & Stigler, J. (2002) A Knowledge Base for the Teaching Profession: what would it look like and how can we get one?, *Educational Researcher*, 31 (5), 3–15.

Higgins, S. & Leat, D. (1997) Horses for Courses or Courses for Horses: what is effective teacher development?, *Journal of In-service Education*, 23 (3), 303–314.

Hodkinson, H. (2009) 'Improving schoolteachers' workplace learning' in S. Gewirtz, P. Mahony, I. Hextall, & A, Cribb, *Changing Teacher Professionalism: International trends, challenges and ways forward*, London: Routledge, pp. 157–169.

Hoyle, E. & John, P. (1995) *Professional Knowledge and Professional Practice*, London: Cassell.

Hufton, N. (2000) Epistemic or Credal Standards for Teachers' Professional Learning and Educational Research – A Common Framework for Inquiry?, *Teachers and Teaching: theory and practice*, 6 (3), 241–257.

Ingersoll, R.M. (2001) *A different approach to solving the teacher shortage problem* (Teaching Quality Policy Brief No. 3). Seattle: University of Washington. Centre for the Study of Teaching and Policy. Retrieved October, 2001, from http://depts.washington.edu/ctpmail.

Ingvarsson, L., Meiers, M. & Beavis, A. (2005) Factors affecting the impact of professional development programs on teachers' knowledge, practice, student outcomes and efficacy, *Education Policy Analysis Archives*, 13 (10), retrieved 4.10.09 from http://epaa.asu.edu/epaa/v13n10/

Jackson, P. (1968) *Life in Classrooms*, Eastbourne: Holt, Rinehart and Winston.

Joint Principals' Association (2006) *Report on Beginning Teachers*, Commissioned by Australian Secondary and Primary Principals' Associations, Unpublished paper.

Keay, J. (2006) What is a PE teacher's role? The influence of learning opportunities on role definition, *Sport, Education and Society*, 11 (4), 369–383.

Keay, J., (2009)Teacher Professional Development: focusing on children's learning,*International Association for Physical Education and Sport for Girls and Women Congress*, South Africa (July, 2009).

Keay, J. & Lloyd, C. (2008a) *Measuring the Impact of Quality Standards on Continuing Professional Development Opportunities in Physical Education and School Sport*, Research Report for Association for Physical Education, UK.

Keay, J. & Lloyd, C. (2008b) *Continuing Professional Development for Talent Development in Physical Education, Monitoring and Evaluation Report, Phase 2*, Report for the Youth Sport Trust.

Keay, J. & Lloyd, C. (2009) High quality professional development in physical education: the role of a subject association, *Professional Development in Education*, 35, (4), 655–676.

Keay, J. & Spence, J. (2010) Resource-Led Professional Development: more than just a marketing tool?, paper presented at *Australian Association for Research in Education Annual Conference*, Melbourne, 27th November-1st December, 2010.

Kemmis, S. (2005) Keynote at Joint International Practitioner Research Conference and the CARN (Collaborative Action Research) Conference, 4–6 November 2005, Utrecht, The Netherlands.

Models of Continuing Professional Development: a framework for analysis, *ice Education*, 31 (2), 235–250.

.. ₍₂₀₀7) Continuing professional development (CPD) policy and the discourse of teacher professionalism in Scotland, *Research Papers in Education*, 22 (1), 95–111.

Kreider, H. & Bouffard, S. (2006) Questions and Answers: A conversation with Thomas R. Guskey, *The Evaluation Exchange*, XI (4), Winter 2005/2006.

Larrivee, B. (2000) Transforming Teaching Practice: becoming the critically reflective teacher, *Reflective Practice*, 1 (3), 293–307.

Law, S. (1999) Leadership for Learning: the changing culture of professional development in schools, *Journal of Education Administration*, 37 (1) [online] available on http://www.emerald-library.com.

Lawless, K.A. & Pelegrino, J.W. (2007) Professional development in integrating technology into teaching and learning: knowns, unknowns, and ways to pursue better questions and answers, *Review of Educational Research*, 71 (4): 575–614.

Leaton Gray, S. (2005) *An Enquiry Into Continuing Professional Development for Teachers*, Cambridge: University of Cambridge and Esmee Fairburn Foundation.

Leitch, S. (2006), *Leitch Review of Skills; Prosperity for All in the Global Economy- World Class Skills*, London: HMSO.

Lloyd, C. (2000) Excellence for all Children – false promises! The failure of current policy for inclusive education and implications for schooling, *International Journal of Inclusive Education*, 4(2), 133–151.

Lloyd, C. (2002), Developing and changing Practice in special educational needs through critically reflective action research: a case study *European Journal of Special Educational Needs*, 17 (2), 109–127.

Lloyd, C. (2008) Removing Barriers to Achievement: A strategy for inclusion or exclusion?, *International Journal of Inclusive Education*, 12(2), pp 221–236.

Lloyd, C. & Beard, J. (1995) *Managing Classroom Collaboration*, London: Cassell.

Lortie, D. (1975) *Schoolteacher*, Chicago, IL: University of Chicago Press.

Lyle, S. (2003) An Investigation Into the impact of a Continuing Professional Development Programme Designed to Support the Development of Teachers as Researchers in South Wales, *Journal of In-Service Education*, 29 (2), 295–312.

MacBeath, J. (1999) *Schools must speak for themselves: the case for school self evaluation*, London: Routledge.

MacDonald Grieve, A. & McGinley, B. (2010) Enhancing professionalism? Teachers' voices on continuing professional development in Scotland, *Teaching Education*, 21 (2), 171–184.

Mahony, P. & Hextall, I. (2009) Building Schools for the Future and its implications for becoming a teacher, paper presented at the *European Conference on Educational Research*, Vienna, 28–30 September, 2009.

Malm, B. (2009) Towards a new professionalism: enhancing personal and professional development in teacher education, *Journal of Education of Teaching*, 35 (1), 77–91.

McCormack, A., Gore, J.M., & Thomas, K. (2004) Learning to teach: Narratives from early career teachers, Paper presented at *AARE Conference, Melbourne*.

McCormick, R., Banks, F., Morgan, B. Opfer, D., Pedder, D., Storey, A. & Wolfenden, F. (2008) *Schools and continuing professional development in England- State of the Nation research project (T34718)*, Report for the Training and Development Agency for Schools: London: TDA.

Mitchell, C. & Sackney, L. (2000) *Profound improvement: capacity building for a learning community*. Lisse: Swets & Zeitlinger.

Morgan, B. (2009) Consulting pupils about teaching and learning: policy, process and response in one school. *Research Papers in Education*, First published on 11th November 2009 (iFirst).

NUT (National Union of Teachers) (2003) The response of the National Union of Teachers to the House of Commons' Education and Skills Committee Inquiry into secondary education teacher retention, NUT.

Novick, R. (1996) Actual Schools Possible Practices: new directions in professional development, *Education Policy Analysis Archives* [online], 14 (4), available from http://epaa.asu.edu/epaa/v4n14.html, [accessed 16.04.99].

Nursing and Midwifery Council (2008) The Code: Standards of conduct, performance and ethics for nurses and midwives, http://www.nmc-uk.org/Nurses-and-midwives/The-code/The-code-in-full/ accessed 29.9.10.

Ofsted (Office for Standards in Education) (2004) *Special Educational Needs and Disability. Towards Inclusive Schools*, London: Ofsted.

Ofsted (Office for Standards in Education) (2006) The logical chain: continuing professional development in effective schools, London: Ofsted HMI.

Ofsted (Office for Standards in Education) (2008) *Early Years, Leading to Excellence*, London, Ofsted.

Oliver, M (1992) Intellectual Masturbation; a rejoinder to Soder and Booth, *European Journal of Special Educational Needs*, 7(1), 20–28.

OECD (Organisation for Economic Cooperation and Development) (2005) *Teachers Matter: Attracting, retaining and developing effective teachers*, Paris: OECD.

Parr, G. (2010) *Inquiry-based professional learning: speaking back to standards-based reforms*, Brisbane: Post Pressed.

Pedder, D., Storey, A. & Opfer, D. (2008) *Schools and continuing professional development in England – State of the Nation research project*, report for TDA.

Perry, P. (1980) Professional Development: the Inspectorate in England and Wales, in E. Hoyle and J. Megarry (Eds.), *World Yearbook of Education 1980, Professional Development of Teachers*, London: Kogan Page, 143–154.

Powell, E., Terry, I., Furey, S. & Scott-Evans, A. (2002) Neglected voices: teachers' perceptions of the impact of continuing professional development, paper presented at *British Educational Research Association* Conference, University of Exeter, 11–14 September.

Pring, R. (2001) Is continuing professional development possible within a centrally controlled education system?, paper presented at *Centre for Policy Studies in Education Seminar*, University of Leeds, 15 March.

Pring, R. (2008) 14–19, *Oxford Review of Education*, 34 (6): 677–688.

Pijl, S. J, Meijer, C. J. W & Hegarty (Eds.) (1997) *Inclusive Education: A Global Agenda*, London: Routledge.

Rogers, C. (1969) *Freedom to Learn*, Ohio: C.E.Merrill.

Rose, R. & Howley, M. (2007) *The Practical Guide to Special Educational Needs in Inclusive Primary Classrooms*, London: Paul Chapman.

Rustemier, S. & Vaughan, M. (2005) *Segregation Trends – LEAs in England 2002–2004*, Bristol: Centre for Studies on Inclusive Education.

Sachs, J. (2001) 'Teacher Professional Identity: competing discourses, competing outcomes', *Journal of Education Policy*, 16 (2), 149–161.

Sachs, J. (2003) *The Activist Teaching Profession*, Buckingham: Open University Press.

Scheerens, J.,Hendriks, M., Luyten, H., Sleegers, P. & Steen, R. (2010)*Teachers' Professional Development - Europe in international comparison — An analysis of teachers' professional development based on the OECD's Teaching and Learning International Survey (TALIS)*, Luxembourg: Office for Official Publications of the European Union.

Schon, D. (1987) *Educating the Reflective Practitioner: toward a new design for teaching and learning in the professions*, New York: Basic Books.

Schulman, L. (1986) Those who understand: knowledge growth in teaching, *Educational Researcher*, 15 (2): 4–14.

Scribner, J. (1999) Professional Development: untangling the influence of work context on teacher learning, *Educational Administration Quarterly*, 35 (2), 238–266.

Slee, R. (2007) It's a Fit-Up ! Inclusive Education, Higher Education, Policy and the Discordant Voice in L. Barton, & F. Armstrong, (2007) *Policy, Experience and Change: Cross Cultural Reflections on Inclusive Education* London: Springer

REFERENCES

Stenhouse, L. (1986), *An Introduction to Curriculum Research and Enquiry*. London: Heinemann.

Strauss A. & Corbin J. (1998) *Basics of Qualitative Research: techniques and procedures for developing grounded theory*, 2nd Edition, London: Sage.

Strong, M. & St. John, L. (2005) A study of teacher retention. The effects of mentoring on beginning teachers, *New Teacher Center*, Santa Cruz, Unpublished paper.

Thomas, G. & James, D. (2006) Reinventing grounded theory: some questions about theory, ground and discovery, *British Educational Research Journal*, 32 (6): 767–795.

Tickle, L. (2000) *Teacher Induction: the way ahead*, Buckingham: Open University Press.

Timmons (2007) Towards Inclusive Education in Canada in Barton, L & Armstrong, F. (2007) *Policy, Experience and Change: Cross Cultural Reflections on Inclusive Education* London: Springer

Timperley, H., Wilson, A. Barrar, H. & Fung, I. (2007) *Teacher Professional Learning and Development, Best Evidence Synthesis Iteration*, New Zealand Ministry of Education.

TDA (Training and Development Agency for Schools) (2007) *PPD Impact Evaluation Report*, London: TDA.

TDA (Training and Development Agency for Schools) (2007) *Professional Standards for Teachers*, London: TDA.

TDA (Training and Development Agency for Schools) (2009) *PPD Impact Evaluation Report, Academic Year 2007/8*, London: TDA.

TDA (Training and Development Agency for Schools) (2009) *Strategy for the professional development of the children's workforce in schools 2009–2012*, Manchester: TDA.

Underwood, J. & Banyard, P. (2008) Managers', teachers' and learners' perceptions of personalised learning: evidence from Impact 2007, *Technology, Pedagogy and Education*, 17 (3): 233–246.

UNESCO (United Nations Educational, Scientific and Cultural Organisation) (1990) *World Declaration on Education for All and Framework for Action to Meet Basic Learning Needs, International Consultative Forum on Education for All*, Paris: UNESCO.

UNESCO (United Nations Educational, Scientific and Cultural Organisation) (1994) *The Salamanca Statement and Framework for Action on Special Needs Education*, Paris: UNESCO.

UNESCO (United Nations Educational, Scientific and Cultural Organisation) (2000) *Dakar Framework for Action – Education for All, meeting our collective commitment*, Paris: UNESCO.

UN (United Nations) (1993) *UN Standard Rules on the Equalisation of Opportunities for Persons with Disabilities*, New York: United Nations.

UN (United Nations) (2006) *Convention of Rights of Persons with Disabilities and Optional Protocol*, New York: United Nations.

Verma, G.K, Bagley, C. R & Mohan, J.H.A. (2007) *International Perspectives on Educational diversity and Inclusion*, London: Routledge.

Warnock, M. (2005) *Special Educational Needs: A New Look*, London: Philosophy Society of Great Britain.

Wenger, E. (1998) *Communities of Practice: learning, meaning and identity*, Cambridge: Cambridge University Press.

Whitehead, M. (2004) Professional Development Board (Physical Education), *British Journal of Teaching Physical Education*, 33 (1), 24.

Williams, C. (2002) Telling Tales: Stories from New Teachers in NSW Country Schools, Paper presented at *AARE Annual Conference. Brisbane.*

Williams, P. (2007) *Ten years on* Higher Quality Bulletin of the QAA for Higher Education No. 24 pp.1–2. Gloucester: QAA.

Williamson, B. & Morgan, J. (2009) Educational reform, enquiry-based learning and the re-professionalisation of teachers, *The Curriculum Journal*, 20 (3), 287–304.

INDEX

INDEX

Lightning Source UK Ltd.
Milton Keynes UK
UKOW05f1607290114

225479UK00001B/10/P

9 789460 916434